The Canadian Spelling Program 2.1

3

Ruth Scott
Sharon Siamon

gage EDUCATIONAL PUBLISHING COMPANY
A DIVISION OF CANADA PUBLISHING CORPORAT
Vancouver · Calgary · Toronto · London ·

Canadian Cataloguing in Publication Data

Scott, Ruth, 1949-
The Canadian spelling program 2.1, 3
Rev. ed.
ISBN 0-7715-1592-8

1. Spellers. 2. English language - Orthography and spelling - Problems, exercises, etc. I. Siamon, Sharon. II. Title.
PE1145.2.S35 1997   428.1   C96-931966-5

Editor: Kim Blakey
Design: Pronk&Associates
Illustration: Dayle Dodwell, Joanne FitzGerald,
          Loris Lesynski, Jackie Snider
Cover Illustration: Jackie Snider

Acknowledgments
The publisher acknowledges the important contribution of Dr. Ves Thomas to *The Canadian Spelling Program* series, in particular the research and development of a uniquely Canadian word list as outlined in his work, *Teaching Spelling*, Second Edition (Gage 1979).

The authors and publisher also acknowledge the contributions of the following educators to *The Canadian Spelling Program 2.1*:

Lynn Archer
Surrey, British Columbia

Caroline Lutyk
Burlington, Ontario

Sylvia Arnold
Aurora, Ontario

Judith MacManus
Riverview, New Brunswick

Halina Bartley
Peterborough, Ontario

Denis Maika
Mississauga, Ontario

Carol Chandler
Halifax, Nova Scotia

Alyson McLelland
Scarborough, Ontario

Jean Hoeft
Calgary, Alberta

Bill Nimigon
North York, Ontario

Lynda Hollowell
North York, Ontario

Gordon Williamson
Winnipeg, Manitoba

ISBN 0-7715-**1592-8**
   5 FP 01 00 99 98
Written, printed, and bound in Canada.

Contents

How to Study Your Words

You will already know how to spell some of the words in this book, but there might be some words that are hard for you.

When you need to study a word, use these steps:

1. **Look** at the word, letter by letter, from beginning to end.

2. **Say** the word to yourself and listen carefully to the sounds.

3. **Cover** the word.

4. **Write** the word.

5. **Check** the spelling, letter by letter, with the word in the list.

If you make a mistake, notice where it is. Did you make a mistake at the beginning of the word, in the middle, or at the end?

Now do all the steps over again with the same word.

Short **a** Short **e**
s**a**t m**e**n

sat
met
fat
bang
set
land
men
said
ten
here
end
ask

See the Words

Look at each word in the list.

Say the Words

1. Say each word. Listen for each sound.

sat fat ask bang land here
met set men ten end said

2. Say the words. Listen for the vowel sounds.

cat   hat   bang

What letter spells the short vowel sound **a** as in **hat**?

3. Say the words. Listen for the vowel sound.

men   ten   net

What letter spells the short vowel sound **e** as in **let**?

✓ Precheck

Check your work. Write the words you misspelled.

★ Powerbooster ★

When we say the vowel sound **a** as in **cat**, we usually spell it with the letter **a**.

When we say the vowel sound **e** as in **ten**, we usually spell it with the letter **e**.

Write the Words

1. a) Read the story.

Once <u>ten</u> of us were on a camping trip. We wanted to know where to <u>set</u> up our tent. At last we <u>met</u> two <u>men</u> who worked in the park. We could <u>ask</u> them!

The men <u>said</u>, "Put your tent up on this piece of flat <u>land</u> over <u>here</u>."

Later my brother Andy blew so much air into his air mattress that it was as <u>fat</u> as a balloon. Then he <u>sat</u> on it. <u>BANG</u>! That was the <u>end</u> of Andy's air mattress.

b) Look for the list words in the story.
Write them in your notebook.

2. Write the list words that have the short **a** sound as in **cat**.

3. Write the list words that have the short **e** sound as in **let**.
Circle the word that spells the short **e** sound with the letters **ai**.

4. Write the list words that fit these boxes.

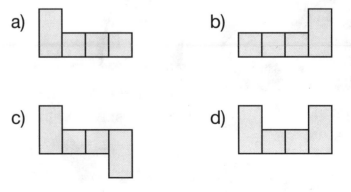

a)

b)

c)

d)

Word Power

1. Use the picture words to make pairs of rhyming words.

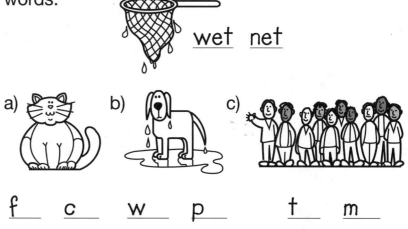

<u>wet</u> <u>net</u>

a)   b)   c)

f___ c___   w___ p___   t___ m___

2. Join each letter in the circles with **et** to make new words.

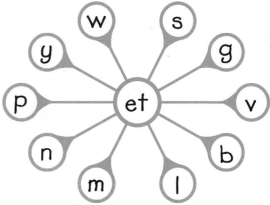

3. a) Look in your math book or your class library for six words with the short **a** sound as in **sat** or the short **e** sound as in **set**. Write three words in each column.

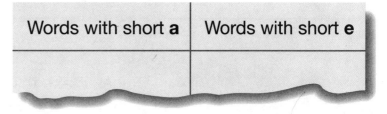

Words with short **a**	Words with short **e**

    b) Choose three of your words. Write a sentence with each word.

SUPER

★ ★ ★ ★ ★

basket
often
pretend
hanger
arrive
engine

★ ★ ★ ★ ★

WORDS

Challenges with Words

1. Solve these riddles. The answers are all Super Words. Write the words.

   a) Use me to hang up your clothes.
      I am a _____ .

   b) I carry things, but I often have holes in me.
      I am a _____ .

   c) When you use your imagination, you _____ .

   d) I mean the opposite of 'to leave'. _____

   e) When something happens a lot, it happens _____ .

   f) A train would be no good without me. _____

2. Complete these sentences with Super Words that fit the boxes. Write the sentences.

   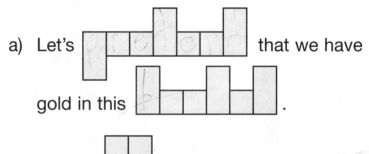

   a) Let's [pretend] that we have gold in this [basket] .

   b) How [often] do the trains [   ] ?

3. Fill in the missing letters in these Super Words. Write the words.

   of _ en   pr _ t _ nd   a _ _ ive

   hang _ r   ba _ _ et   _ ng _ n _

4. Engines make things like cars and trucks go. Make a list of things that have engines.

   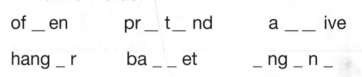

   Example   train, snowmobile

4

5. Let's pretend! Choose a character from the box below. Then, choose an event that happens to your character from the second box. You can also make up your own character and event. Write the character and the event you choose in your notebook.

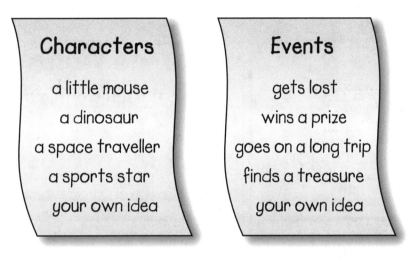

Characters

a little mouse

a dinosaur

a space traveller

a sports star

your own idea

Events

gets lost

wins a prize

goes on a long trip

finds a treasure

your own idea

6. a) Write a story about what happens to your character. You might want to begin your story like this:

One day...   or   Once upon a time...

b) Share your story by reading it to a partner.

7. Complete the story with Kids Words. Write the story in your notebook.

One day, Joanne put her baseball _____ on her head, and her _____ on her back. "Wait!" said her big brother. "Don't forget your bike _____."

Kids WORDS

pack

cap

helmet

2 Short i
bit

ever
sick
well
dragon
hill
woods
tell
pick
smell
because
kill
bit

See the Words

Look at each word in the list.

Say the Words

1. Say each word. Listen for each sound.

   hill   kill   sick   pick   bit

   well   tell   smell   ever

   dragon   because   woods

2. Say the words. Listen for the vowel sounds.

   hill   mitt   fish

What letter spells the short vowel sound **i** as in **it**?

☑ **Precheck**

Check your work. What words do you need to study?

★ **Powerbooster** ★

When we say the short vowel sound **i** as in **hill** and **bit**, we usually spell it with the letter **i**.

Write the Words

1. a) Read this list of hiking rules.

Have you <u>ever</u> gone hiking in the <u>woods</u>?
Here are some things to remember if you do.
1. <u>Tell</u> someone where you are going.
2. Make sure your path is <u>well</u> marked.
3. Don't make a fire <u>because</u> forest fires <u>kill</u> plants and animals.
4. <u>Smell</u> all the flowers you like, but just <u>pick</u> a few.
5. Don't eat any leaves or berries off the trees. They could make you <u>sick</u>.
6. Always clean up your camp <u>site</u>.
   The last <u>bit</u> to remember is this — have fun!

b) Look for the list words in the rules above. Write them in your notebook.

c) Which two list words are left out?
d _ _ _ _ n   h _ _ l

Write a sentence with each of these words.

2. Write the list words that have the short **i** sound as in **it**.

3. Write the list words that have the short **e** sound as in **let**.

4. Write the list words that fit these boxes.

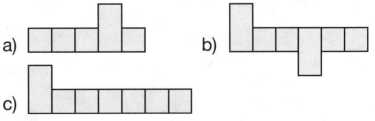

a)

b)

c)

Word Power

1. Find the missing words. Write the sentences.

   a) I used to be <u>s</u> _ _ <u>k</u> , but now I am .

   b) Let's <u>p</u> _ _ <u>k</u> some  .

2. Complete each set of words. Write the list word that goes with the other two words.

   a) taste   hear   _____
   b) say   speak   _____
   c) dinosaur   monster   _____
   d) forest   trees   _____

3. a) Write these headings in your book.

Short **e** as in **let**	Short **i** as in **it**

   b) Now write each short **e** and short **i** word under the correct heading.

fill	file	fell	felt	feel
let	wet	win	bit	find
in	mend	mind	left	lift

4. Complete the sentence below using words of your own. Write the sentence in your notebook.

   My favourite season is _____
   because _____ .

8

SUPER
★ ★ ★ ★ ★
habit
ribbon
trust
film
nickel
silver
★ ★ ★ ★ ★
WORDS

Challenges with Words

1. Write the Super Words that fit each of the boxes.

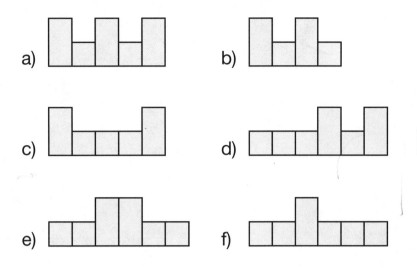

a)

b)

c)

d)

e)

f)

2. Complete the sentences with Super Words. Write the words.

a) Exercising is a good h _ _ _ _ _ .

b) Jenny won a r _ _ _ _ _ _ in the contest.

c) I t _ _ _ _ you because you are my friend.

d) Don't forget to put f _ _ _ in your camera.

3. Answer these questions about nickels. Write your answers in sentences.

a) How many nickels make a quarter?

b) How many nickels make a loony?

c) What picture is on the back of a nickel?

4. Write your own fill-in-the-blank sentences with the words **nickel**, **silver**, and **film**. Trade your sentences with a partner.

5. Write the picture words. They all have the letters **ck** in the middle.

a)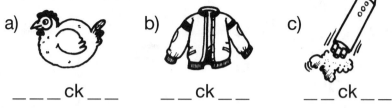

_ _ _ ck _ _

b)

_ _ ck _ _

c)

_ _ ck _ _

6. Solve the puzzle! Find the word that fits this sentence. Use the clues below to find each letter.

Silver _ _ _ _ _ _ very brightly.

__ is a letter in **silver**, but not in **deliver**

__ is a letter in **habit**, but not in **rabbit**

__ is a letter in **film**, but not in **flame**

__ is a letter in **nickel**, but not in **tickle**

__ is a letter in **test**, but not in **trust**

__ is a letter in **robins**, but not in **ribbon**

7. a) Imagine you have a camera. Talk with a partner about what kinds of pictures you would like to take.

b) Find a picture of yourself. Describe how old you were when the picture was taken, what you were doing, and where you were.

3

Short **o**

st**o**p

stop
cows
pond
class
best
trip
leg
rock
left
they
girl
top

✓ Precheck

Check your work. Underline the parts of the words you need to study.

See the Words

Look at each word in the list.

Say the Words

1. Say each word. Listen for each sound.

top stop rock pond best leg left

girl trip they cows class

2. Say the words. Listen for the vowel sounds.

stop   rock   dog

What letter spells the short **o** sound as in **hot**?

★ Powerbooster ★

When we say the short vowel sound **o** as in **top** and **stop**, we usually spell it with the letter **o**.

Write the Words

1. **a)** Read the story.

> Last week our <u>class</u> took a field <u>trip</u> that we will never forget! First, we <u>left</u> the picnic basket at school. No lunch! Then a <u>girl</u> climbed to the <u>top</u> of a <u>rock</u> cliff. A <u>boy</u> fell and hurt his <u>leg</u>. Finally some kids got chased by <u>cows</u>. The kids couldn't <u>stop</u>. <u>They</u> ran right into the duck <u>pond</u>. All in all it wasn't the <u>best</u> field trip we ever had.

b) Look for the list words in the story. Write them in your notebook.

In a **blend** the two consonants are sounded together. **st**art **cr**y

2. Write the list words that have the short **o** sound as in **hot**.

3. Write these words in your notebook. Circle the consonant blend in each word.

stop   pond   class   best   trip   left

4. Write the list words that fit the boxes.

a) Vicki and Manjit are wet because

fell in the   .

b) Our neighbours have two boys and one

.

c) The farmer tripped and hurt his   when

he was milking the   .

Word Power

Hint! When I **trip** I fall. When I take a **trip** I go on a journey.

1. Some of the list words have more than one meaning. Write the list words that match these meanings.

   a) to fall; a journey t _ _ p
   b) the opposite of bottom; a toy that spins t _ p
   c) a large stone; to move back and forth r _ _ k
   d) the opposite of right; what remains l _ _ t

2. Write the correct list word for each question.

   a) What is the opposite of **go**?

pots	spot
stop	tops

   b) What is the opposite of **worst**?

test	best
sets	bets

3. Complete the sentences with words that spell the short **o** sound with the letter **o**.

   a) We saw a f r _ _ at the p _ _ _ _ .

   b) How much does a h _ t   d _ g
      c _ _ _ ?

   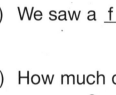

   c) Kim scored a goal in the
      h _ _ _ e y game.

   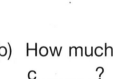

4. a) Write about the best class trip you have ever had. Use as many list words as you can.

   b) Trade stories with a partner. Can you suggest ways to make it better?

13

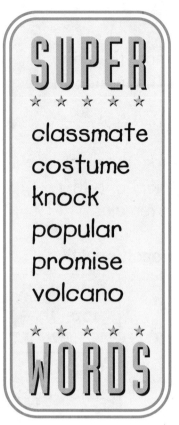

Challenges with Words

1. Use the clues to solve these riddles. The answers are all Super Words.

a) This word could mean the person sitting beside you. _____

b) You should never break one of these. _____

c) When a lot of people like something it is _____ .

d) When you dress up as someone else, you are wearing a _____ .

e) You do this on a door. _____

f) A mountain that smokes is called a _____ .

2. Write the Super Words in alphabetical order.

a) When two words begin with the same letter, look at the second letter.

Example **ca**ke **cl**imb

3. Complete these sentences with Super Words. Write the sentences in your notebook.

a) The clown was very p _ _ _ _ _ _ in his bright c _ _ _ _ _ _ _ .

b) I p _ _ _ _ _ _ _ to k _ _ _ _ before coming in.

c) Mina is my new c _ _ _ _ _ _ _ _ _ .

4. Write the Super Words that complete the sets.

a) trust   secret   _____

b) clothes   disguise   _____

c) mountain   lava   _____

5. The Super Word **knock** has a silent **k**. Each of the picture words also has a silent **k**. Write the words.

kn _ _   kn _ _ _   kn _ _   kn _ _ _ _

6. Have you heard this knock-knock joke?

Knock, knock.
Who's there?
Ken.
Ken who?
Ken you come out to play?

Write your own knock-knock joke. Try it on your friends.

7. Copy the words below. Underline the words that have the short **o** sound as in **top**.

| hockey | law | cough | come |
| cauliflower | water | shoe | automatic |

8. Unscramble the words to complete these sentences.

a) The gof was so thick I could hardly see.

b) The mogs made my eyes sting.

c) Clean air would be a wonderful tgif !

Hint! There are five ways to spell short **o**.

Kids
WORDS

fog
smog
gift

Short **u**
d**u**ck

runs
visit
under
gets
duck
still
wind
jumps
egg
just
last
until

See the Words

Look at each word in the list.

Say the Words

1. Say each word. Listen for each sound.

runs   jumps   under   until

duck   just   still   wind

visit   gets   egg   last

2. Say the words. Listen for the vowel sounds.

runs   jumps   duck

What letter spells the short **u** sound as in **cup**?

☑ Precheck

**Check your work.
Write the words
you misspelled.**

★ Powerbooster ★

When we say the short vowel sound **u** as in **up**
and **cup**, we usually spell it with the letter **u**.

Write the Words

1. a) Read the story.

Every day I <u>visit</u> my <u>duck</u> Snowball as she sits on her six eggs. She is keeping the eggs warm <u>under</u> her body. Even when the <u>wind</u> is cold her soft warm feathers protect her eggs. She doesn't like Brio the dog because he <u>runs</u> and <u>jumps</u> around her nest.

I <u>just</u> can't wait <u>until</u> the <u>last</u> <u>egg</u> hatches. I'm sure Snowball <u>gets</u> tired of waiting too. She has to sit so <u>still</u> on her nest!

b) Look for the list words in the story.
Write them in your notebook.

2. Write the six list words that have the short **u** sound as in **cup**.

3. Write the two list words that end in double consonants. Circle the double consonants.

Look for two consonants that are the same.

4. Write the list words that fit the boxes.

a) We played ☐☐☐☐ bedtime.

b) Their dog crawled ☐☐☐☐ my bed.

c) The ☐☐☐☐ blew hard ☐☐☐☐ night.

Word Power

1. Complete each verse with the list word that rhymes. Write the words in your notebook.

   a) If you run very fast,
      You won't come in _____.

   b) A camel has humps,
      But a kangaroo _____ .

   c) If you are ill,
      You must lie very _____ .

2. The vowels have been taken out of these list words. Write the words in your notebook.

   r _ ns   v _ s _ t   _ gg   _ nt _ l

   w _ nd   st _ ll   g _ ts   l _ st

Remember! The vowels are **a e i o u** and sometimes **y**.

3. Say the words below. Write the words that have the short **u** sound as in **cup**.

funny	stuck	super
button	thunder	soup

4. Complete this sentence using the picture clues. Write the words.

   Andrew   home,   into   ,

   and hides   the blankets.

5. What do you think makes Andrew do these strange things? Write a sentence about it.

SUPER
★ ★ ★ ★ ★
unhappy
underwater
runway
duckling
visitor
thunder
★ ★ ★ ★ ★
WORDS

tooth | brush

Challenges with Words

1. Write these Super Words. Underline the base word in each.

   unhappy   duckling   visitor

2. Complete each set with a Super Word. Write the Super Words.

   a) sad   sorry   _____

   b) chick   gosling   _____

   c) driveway   laneway   _____

   d) rain   lightning   _____

3. Have you ever seen a thunderstorm? Write **thunder** as a key word then build as many storm words as you can. One has been done for you.

   ```
          w
          i
   t h u n d e r
          d
   ```

4. Write the two Super Words that are compounds. Draw a box around each of the small words.

5. The word part **un-** means 'not'. For example, **unhappy** means 'not happy'. Write words beginning with **un-** that mean the same as the words below.

   a) sad means   un _ _ _ _ _

   b) raw means   un _ _ _ _ _ _ _

   c) cruel means   un _ _ _ _ _

6. Here's a riddle to solve. Write the answer.

Q. What does a duckling eat underwater?

A. A s _ b _ _ r _ _ e s _ _ d w _ _ h !

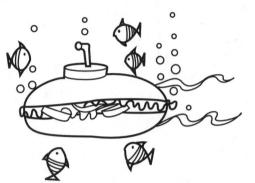

7. a) Talk with a partner or small group about some underwater adventures you might have if you were a diver. Jot down your ideas.

b) Write a story about one of your adventures. Draw a picture to go with your story.

5

Long a
a _ e
lake

game
much
lake
trunk
snake
skunk
sing
friend
king
people
same
gave

✓ Precheck

Check your work. Underline the parts of the words you need to study.

See the Words

Look at each word in the list.

Say the Words

1. Say each word. Listen for each sound.

game   same   lake   snake

gave   much   skunk   trunk

sing   king   friend   people

2. Say the words. Listen for the vowel sounds.

snake   wave   cane

What letters spell the long **a** sound as in **age**?

★ Powerbooster ★

The long **a** sound is often spelled with the letters **a _ e** as in **lake**.

Write the Words

1. a) Read the story.

I have a <u>friend</u> who <u>gave</u> me a new <u>game</u>. I like it very <u>much</u>. It's not the <u>same</u> as my other games. <u>People</u> have to act like the animals the spinner points to. For example:

- If you land on a <u>snake</u>—crawl on the floor.
- If you land on a <u>skunk</u>—hold your nose.
- If you land on a <u>bird</u>—<u>sing</u> a song.
- If you land on a lion—roar like the <u>king</u> of the beasts.
- If you land on a fish—pretend you're swimming in a <u>lake</u>.
- If you land on an elephant—swing your arms like a <u>trunk</u>.

b) Look for the list words in the story. Write them in your notebook.

2. Write the list words that have the long **a** sound as in **age**.

3. Write the four pairs of rhyming words.

4. Write the word **friend**. Circle the letters that spell the short **e** sound.

5. Write the list words that fit these boxes.

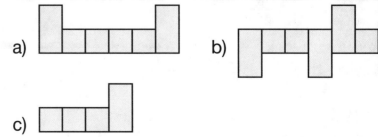

a)

b)

c)

Remember! Words that rhyme often end with the same letters.
sing   king

22

Word Power

1. Solve these riddles. The answers are list words. Write the words.

a) I slither along
   Without any sound.
   I am a _____ .

b) I laugh when you're happy
   And cry when you're sad.
   I am your _____ .

2. Write new words by changing the circled letters.

a) g a (m) e   g a t e   _ _ v _   _ _ z _
b) s a (m) e   _ _ f _   _ _ l _   _ _ v _
c) t a (m) e   _ _ k _   _ _ l _   _ _ p _

3. Complete these sentences with list words. Write the sentences.

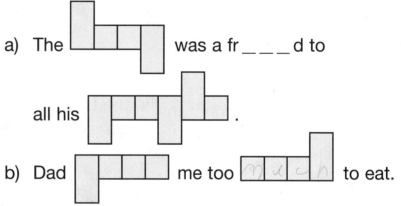

a) The [ ] was a fr _ _ _ d to

   all his [ ] .

b) Dad [ ] me too much to eat.

4. a) What is a friend? Write about your friends and what makes them special to you. Use the sentence frame to get you started.

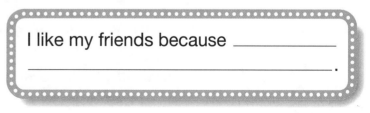

I like my friends because _____
_____.

b) Paint or draw a picture to go with your sentence.

SUPER WORDS

girlfriend
bakery
spaceship
safety
basement
brave

Challenges with Words

1. Write the Super Words that have the long **a** sound as in **age**. Underline the base words.

2. Complete these sentences with Super Words. Write the words.

a) We buy bread at the _____.

b) The _____ circled Earth.

c) Renee's _____ is coming to play.

d) Always obey the _____ rules.

e) Our toys are in the _____.

3. Write the two Super Words that are compounds. Put a box around the two small words that make each compound word.

4. a) Make words with the word wheel. Write the words.

b) Write a verse with some of the words.

5. Add the word **ship** to the beginning or end of these words. Write the new compound words.

friend	wreck	mate
builder	steam	yard

6. Match the compound words you wrote in exercise 5 with these definitions. Write the definitions and words.

  a) someone whose job is making ships
  b) being friends
  c) a place where ships are built
  d) someone who works with you on a ship
  e) a sunken ship

7. a) Are the children playing safely in this picture? Look carefully. Write about three things that are not safe.

  b) Share your writing with a group. Does everyone in the group agree?

8. Write the words that fit the shapes below.

She was [ ][ ][ ][ ] before seven o'clock.

She looked at the [ ][ ][ ][ ] on the calendar.

She hoped her holiday would be exciting,

not [ ][ ][ ][ ] !

6

STUDY STEPS

look

say

cover

write

check

Looking Back

Here is a list of words from Units 1–5 that may be hard for you.

1. Use the Study Steps for each word. Your teacher will dictate the words.

2. Write the picture words by filling in the vowels.

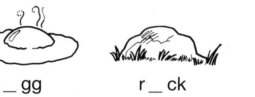

a) _ gg   r _ ck   d _ ck

b) gl _ ss   l _ k _   t _ nt

c) dr _ g _ n   h _ ll   st _ p

d) sn _ k _   w _ ndm _ ll   sk _ nk

26

3. Read the picture sentences.
Write the sentences in words.

a)

b) went to the

c) The and the live in the

d) The made friends with the

4. Some words in these sentences have lost their
vowels. Use the vowel sound in each word clue
to help you complete the sentences.

a) **cup.** My dog rns and jmps ntil it's time to
eat lnch.
b) **age.** We plyed the sm gm at the lk.
c) **it.** See f the toy s n the bg box.
d) **let.** This is the bst tnt we have.
e) **hat.** Tht bng made our ct jump.
f) **hot.** Stp at the tp f the hill.

5. Choose a word to fit each sentence.
Write the words.

a) Farmers grow wheat on this _____ .

> hand land
> sand band

b) Last night we slept in a _____ .

> went bent
> tent sent

c) How many berries did you _____ ?

> trick sick
> kick pick

d) Have you ever played this _____ ?

> game same
> name lame

6. Make six headings in your notebook like this.
Find three more words in classroom books to write under each heading.

short a	short e	short i	short o	short u	long a
hat	let	it	hot	cup	age

7. Make your own review list. Use words that you misspelled on the Unit Tests.
Add words from your own writing and your Personal Word List.

Follow the five Study Steps for each word.

Fall

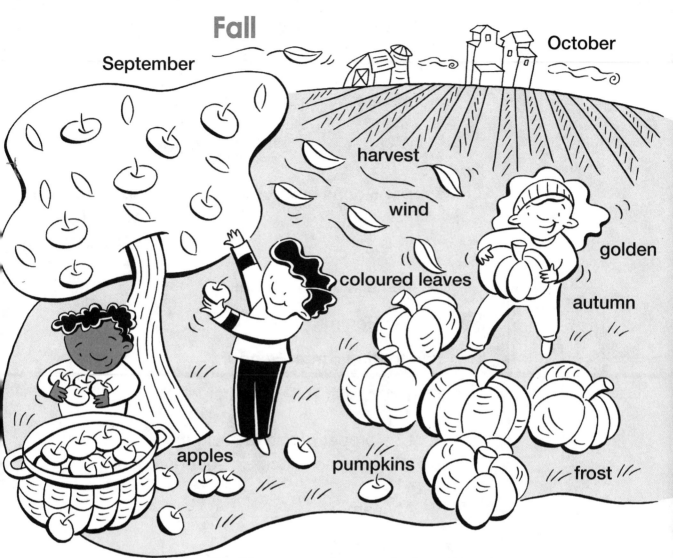

September

October

harvest

wind

coloured leaves

golden

autumn

apples

pumpkins

frost

1. These words are all about the fall. You and your classmates will be able to add many other words to your class list.

2. Write a sentence that explains why you like fall.

I like fall because _____

_____ .

3. Write a letter to someone who lives in a warm climate. Describe what the fall season is like in Canada.

Grammar Games

Nouns

Nouns are words that name **people**
          places
          things

Proper Nouns are words that name **special people**
               special places
               special things

My name is **Jessie Jones**.

I live in **Regina**.

I go to **Pine Street School**.

My birthday is in **September**.

1. Use proper nouns to finish these sentences.
   Write the sentences in your notebook.

   My name is _____ _____ .

   I live in _____ .

   I go to _____ .

   My birthday is in _____ .

2. Write the words in the list below that are proper
   nouns.

fall	Canada	Monday	desk	Waldo
happy	October	finger	Calgary	pen

Dictionary Games

In a dictionary the words are in alphabetical order. For example, the words that begin with **a** come before the words that begin with **b**.

1. Look at the words in the picture below. Write them in alphabetical order.

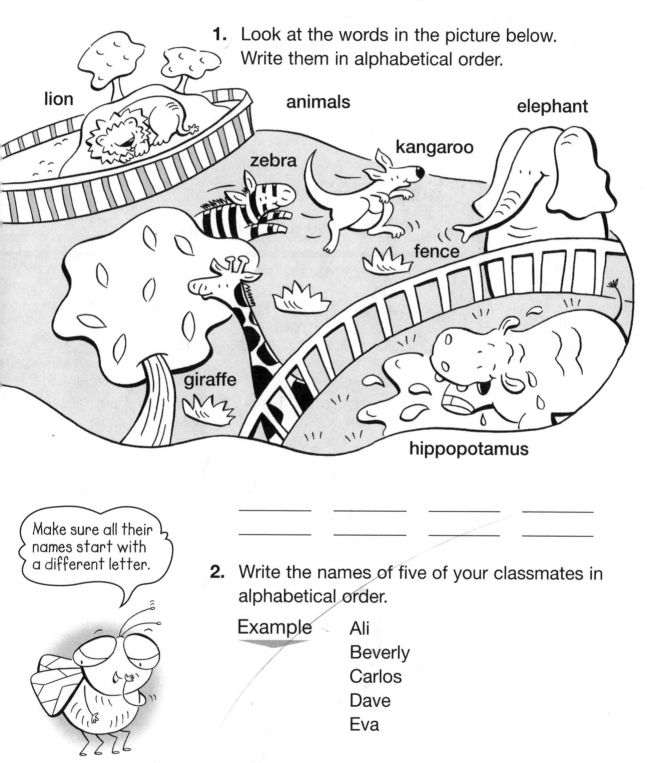

lion

animals

elephant

kangaroo

zebra

fence

giraffe

hippopotamus

Make sure all their names start with a different letter.

____ ____ ____ ____

____ ____ ____ ____

2. Write the names of five of your classmates in alphabetical order.

Example   Ali
            Beverly
            Carlos
            Dave
            Eva

7

Long e
ee
f**ee**t

feet
looks
asleep
books
queen
teeth
first
games
street
every
ago
about

See the Words

Look at each word in the list.

Say the Words

1. Say each word. Listen for each sound.

feet	street	asleep	teeth
queen	first	books	looks
ago	about	every	games

2. Say the words. Listen for the vowel sounds.

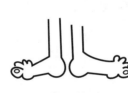

feet

asleep

tree

What letters spell the long **e** sound as in **me**?

✓ Precheck

**Check your work.
What words do
you need to study?**

★ Powerbooster ★

The long **e** sound is often spelled with the letters
ee as in **sheep** and **teeth**.

Write the Words

1. a) Read the story.

Every year the kids on Queen Street have a dress-up contest. First prize goes to the kid who looks most like someone who lived long ago. This year I was Dracula. I looked in books to read about how he dressed. I had a long cape and wore black boots on my feet. I had a set of make-believe teeth.

The night before the contest, I was so excited I couldn't fall asleep.

I had a lot of fun the next day dressing up and playing games with the other kids.

b) Look for the list words in the story. Write them in your notebook.

2. Write the list words with the long **e** sound spelled **ee**.

> Words that rhyme sound the same.

3. Write the two pairs of list words that rhyme.

4. Write the list words that fit these boxes.

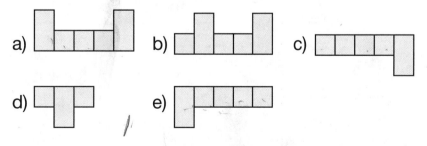

a)

b)

c)

d)

e)

Word Power

1. Use the clues to write words that have the long **e** sound spelled **ee**.

   a) the colour of grass is gr _ _ n
   b) seven days make one w _ _ k
   c) you walk on them f _ _ t
   d) its leaves turn colours in the fall tr _ _
   e) each plant begins as a s _ _ d

2. Complete each sentence with list words. Write the words.

   a) I ran down the s _ _ _ _ _ _ in bare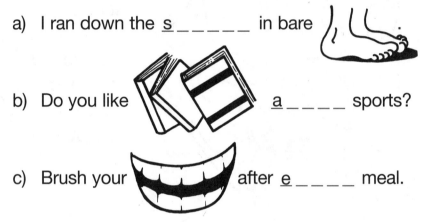

   b) Do you like a _ _ _ _ _ sports?

   c) Brush your after e _ _ _ _ meal.

Plural means more than one. One **mouse** Two **mice**

3. Make each word mean **more than one**. Write the pairs of words in your notebook.

   foot   tooth   goose   mouse

4. Write a word that rhymes with each of these list words.

   feet   looks   queen   games

5. Work with a partner. Write a silly rhyme using your rhyming words from exercise 4.

   My sister looks at
    picture books.

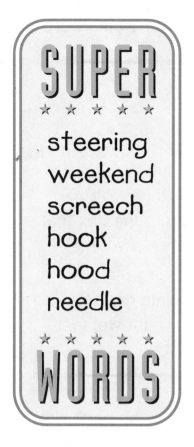

SUPER WORDS

steering
weekend
screech
hook
hood
needle

Challenges with Words

1. Complete the sentences with Super Words. Write the words.

   a) Last _____ we visited my uncle.
   b) I heard the tires _____ and then there was a crash.
   c) The driver turned the _____ wheel.
   d) The point on the fish _____ was as sharp as a _____.
   e) My jacket has a warm _____.

2. Hook the letters on the fish to **ook** and **ood** to make new words. Write the words.

3. a) Complete the puzzle with Super Words. Write them in your notebook.

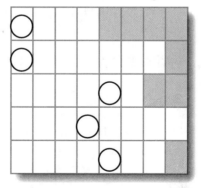

   a) found on a jacket or a car
   b) Saturday and Sunday
   c) used for sewing
   d) handlebars are used for _____
   e) sounds like a scream

   b) Unscramble the circled letters to find an important car part.   W _____

4. Write a sentence with each of the **noise** words.

    a) screech

    b) scream

    c) squeal

5. Write as many small words as you can using the letters in **steering**.

6. Fill in the blanks with words from the box that end with **le**. Write the sentences in your notebook.

    a) The compass _____ points north.

    b) I stepped in a _____ and got wet feet.

    c) The rider climbed up into the _____ .

    d) We boiled water in the _____ .

saddle
puddle
needle
kettle

7. Draw a picture of a car. Label all the parts like **door** and **bumper**.

8. Imagine you are driving to a beautiful lake to go fishing and swimming.

    a) List some of the things you see, hear, and smell.

    b) Write a story about your trip. Use as many Super Words as you can.

9. Write the words that match the clues below.

    a) A _ _ _ _ _ _ _ is a nose explosion.

    b) You may have to pay a _ _ _ when you sign up for a team.

    c) _ _ _ _ _ _ is the opposite of disagree.

Kids WORDS

agree
sneeze
fee

8

Long **a** Short **o**
ay **a**
pl**ay** f**a**ll

may
stay
also
Sunday
fall
week
Saturday
cave
holiday
small
always
almost

See the Words

Look at each word in the list.

Say the Words

1. Say each word. Listen for each sound.

   may   stay   Saturday   Sunday

   holiday   cave   always   almost

   also   fall   small   week

2. Say the words. Listen for the vowel sounds.

   may   holiday   Sunday   play

   What letters spell the long **a** sound as in **age**?

3. Say the words. Listen for the first vowel sounds.

   always   almost   also

   What letter spells the short **o** sound as in **hot**?

☑ Precheck

**Check your work.
Write the words
you misspelled.**

★ Powerbooster ★

The long **a** sound as in **cake** is often spelled with the letters **ay**.

The short **o** sound as in **ball** is often spelled with the letter **a**.

35

Write the Words

1. a) Read the story.

On our <u>holiday</u> we <u>always</u> go to my aunt's house. This year we <u>may</u> <u>stay</u> for a <u>week</u>. We'll leave on <u>Saturday</u> and come home next <u>Sunday</u>. We <u>also</u> plan to visit the caves again. Last <u>fall</u> we explored a <u>small</u> <u>cave</u> that was full of bats! They flew out when we shone our flashlight around the cave. I <u>almost</u> dropped the light! It was really exciting.

b) Look for the list words in the story.
Write them in your notebook.

Some vowel sounds can be spelled with more than one letter.

2. Write the five list words that have the short **o** sound as in **hot** spelled with the letter **a**.

3. Write the seven list words that have the long **a** sound as in **age**. Circle the words that spell the long **a** sound with **ay**.

4. Write the list words that fit the boxes.

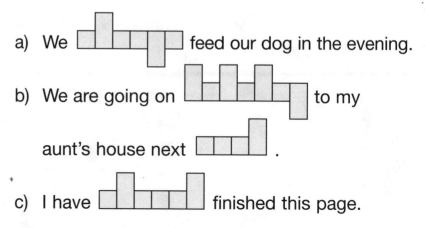

a) We ⬚⬚⬚⬚⬚ feed our dog in the evening.

b) We are going on ⬚⬚⬚⬚⬚⬚ to my

aunt's house next ⬚⬚⬚⬚ .

c) I have ⬚⬚⬚⬚⬚⬚ finished this page.

Word Power

See how many other list words you can use in your sentences.

1. Three of the list words begin with the letters **al**. Write your own sentences with these words.

2. Each picture word has the short **o** sound spelled with the letter **a**. Write the words.

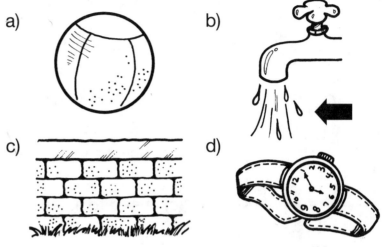

a)

b)

c)

d)

3. Join the letters with **ay**. Write new words that rhyme with **play**.

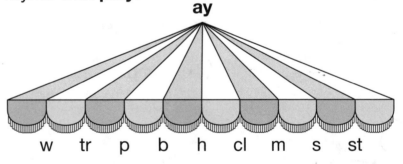

ay

w   tr   p   b   h   cl   m   s   st

4. Write the days of the week. Remember to use a capital letter at the beginning of each word.

5. Write sentences using each pair of words.

holiday / week

stay / always

SUPER
★ ★ ★ ★ ★

railway
highway
passengers
dangerous
radio
washed

★ ★ ★ ★ ★
WORDS

Hint! If two words have the same first and second letter, look at the third letter.

Challenges with Words

1. Write the Super Words that match these clues.

   a) two compound words
   b) three words with three syllables
   c) a word that spells short **o** as in **hot** with **a**
   d) two words that spell long **a** as in **age** with **ay**

2. Find a Super Word that goes with each clue. Write the words.

   a) people who travel on planes and trains

      — — — — — — — — — —

   b) never play on this road

      — — — — — — — —

   c) used to listen to music

      — — — — —

   d) train tracks _ _ _ _ _ _ _ _

   e) opposite of safe _ _ _ _ _ _ _ _ _ _

3. Write the Super Words in alphabetical order.

4. Complete each set of words with a Super Word. Write the answers.

   a) tracks   engine   conductor _____

   b) television CD player cassette _____

   c) riders   travellers people _____

   d) risky   difficult   unsafe _____

   e) cleaned   dried   rinsed _____

   f) road   street   expressway _____

5. A few words end with the letter **o**. Write the words that fit each sentence.

a) We listened to a story on the r _ _ _ o .

b) We watched the cowhands at the r _ _ _ o .

c) The p _ _ _ _ o is a vegetable that grows under the ground.

d) The b _ _ _ _ _ o is a very large wild animal of the Prairies.

6. What goes up but never comes down?
Use this code to write the answer.

1	2	3	4	5	6	7	8	9	10	11	12	13
X	K	Y	L	Z	M	A	N	B	O	C	P	D

14	15	16	17	18	19	20	21	22	23	24	25	26
Q	E	R	F	S	G	T	H	U	I	V	J	W

3 10 22 16   7 19 15

— — — —   — — — !

7. Use the code from exercise 6 to write this message in code.

> DANGEROUS FLOODS.
> RAILWAY BLOCKED.

8. a) Write an adventure story where you have to send the message from exercise 7. Use as many Super Words as you can.

b) Proofread your story with a partner.

9

Long i
i _ e
bite

side
times
our
high
bite
kept
felt
tired
where
inside
wild
upon

See the Words

Look at each word in the list.

Say the Words

1. Say each word. Listen for each sound.

   side   inside   times   tired   bite   wild

   high   kept   felt   where   our   upon

2. Say the words. Listen for the vowel sounds.

   side   nice   times   tired   bite

   What letters spell the long **i** sound as in **ice**?

Check your work. Underline the parts of the words you need to study.

★ **Powerbooster** ★

In some words we use the letters **i__e** to spell the long **i** sound as in **ice**.

Write the Words

1. a) Read the story.

Once upon a time there was a school where the children kept arguing with each other. At times the arguing got very loud and wild. Then someone would always go inside to tell the teacher.

One day, a girl named Rozika said, "I'm tired of this! It's high time we learned how to settle our problems. Let's make some rules."

So they decided it was not fair to yell at each other. If two kids felt they couldn't stop arguing, they would ask someone to help solve the problem without taking one side or the other. Soon the schoolyard was a much more peaceful place.

b) Write the list words from the story.
c) Write the list word that is not in the story.
   b ＿ ＿ e.

2. Write the list words that have the long **i** sound spelled **i ＿ e**.

3. Write the two list words that have the short **e** sound as in **let**.

4. Complete the sentences with list words that fit the boxes. Write the words.

a) Ask Dad ⬚⬚⬚⬚ ⬚⬚⬚ toys are.

b) Once ⬚⬚⬚⬚ a time, there lived a very kind woman.

Word Power

Hint! These words make me think about being **tired**.

1. Complete each set with a list word. Write the words.

a) sleepy   drowsy   _____

b) his   her   _____

c) outside   beside   _____

c) chew   nibble   _____

2. Write words that spell long **i** with the letters **i __ e**.

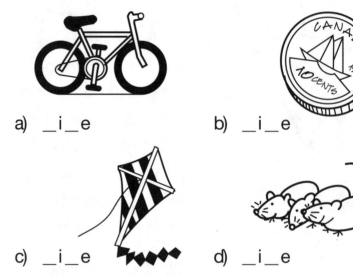

a) _ i _ e   b) _ i _ e

c) _ i _ e   d) _ i _ e

Here are your question words.
Why   When
What   Where

3. Complete the sentences with the question words. Write the sentences in your notebook.

Why   When   What   Where

a) _____ are the monkeys?

b) _____ are they hiding in the trees?

c) _____ is their feeding time?

d) _____ do they eat?

4. Write questions of your own using the question words **where** and **when**.

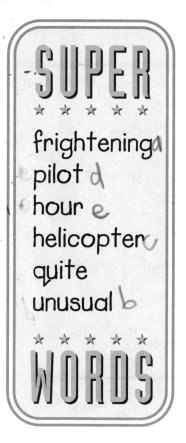

SUPER WORDS

frightening a
pilot d
hour e
helicopter c
quite
unusual b

Challenges with Words

1. Find the Super Word that fits each box. Write the words in your notebook.

a) h e l i c o p t e r

b) p i

c) f r i g h t e n i n g

d)

2. Complete each sentence with a Super Word. Write the words.

a) The movie about pirates was very _____ .

b) Hot weather is _____ in January.

c) A _____ is a special kind of aircraft.

d) The _____ landed the plane safely.

e) Sixty minutes makes one _____.

3. Find a word in the box that fits each sentence. Write the words in your notebook.

Lots of words make the opposite by adding **un**. I **tie** my shoes and I **untie** them.

undone	undress	uncooked
unusual	untie	unlucky

a) I can't _____ this knot.

b) If you never win a prize you are _____ .

c) Salads are usually _____ .

d) What you do before bed. _____

e) Oh! My jacket is _____ .

f) We saw an _____ object in the sky.

4. Say these words. Write the number of syllables you hear in each one.

   a) unusual   b) helicopter   c) frightening

5. Look at these pictures. Write about what is unusual in each one.

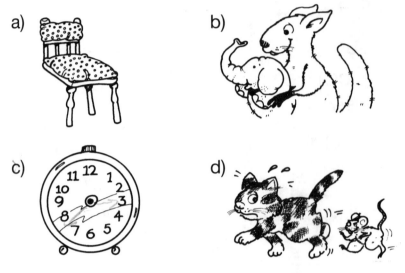

a)

b)

c)

d)

6. Write the three Super Words that have the long **i** sound. Underline the letters that spell long **i**.

7. Imagine you are a pilot. Complete the sentences with Super Words. Write the rest of the story.

I am a _____ . One day, something very _____ happened. Suddenly, six _____ strange objects surrounded my _____ . An _____ later …

8. Here are some words about going out to eat. Unscramble the words to complete the sentences.

   a) "Let's go out for dinner ginthot!" said Sandi.
   b) The crepi for the soup and salad combo was very low.
   c) Mom said I put too much lsta on my food.

Kids
WORDS

price
tonight
salt

10

-ing Ending
do**ing**

doing
getting
ate
morning
later
sitting
camping
maybe
running
looking
soft
fire

See the Words

1. Look at each word in the list.

2. Look at these words. Notice the base words.

run running   get getting   hop hopping

The base words all end in one vowel and one consonant. What happens when we add **-ing** to these base words?

Say the Words

Say each word in the list. Listen for each sound.

running   getting   camping   looking

doing   morning   sitting

later   ate   maybe   soft   fire

✓ Precheck

Check your work. Write the words you misspelled.

★ Powerbooster ★

When a base word ends in one short vowel and one consonant, double the final consonant before adding **-ing** as in **get + t + ing** and **run + n + ing**.

Write the Words

1. a) Read the story.

> We loved <u>camping</u> in the woods last summer. We loved <u>getting</u> up early in the <u>morning</u> and <u>running</u> down to the lake to wash our faces. We loved staying up late, <u>sitting</u> by the <u>fire</u>, <u>looking</u> at the flames, and then falling asleep on a <u>soft</u> camp bed. We even liked <u>doing</u> the camp dishes after we <u>ate</u>. My parents said <u>maybe</u> we'll go camping <u>later</u> this summer.

b) Look for the list words in the story.
Write them in your notebook.

> A base word is the part of a word that stands alone, like **get** in **get**ting.

2. Write the list words that end in **-ing**. Underline the base words that end in one vowel and one consonant.

3. Write the list words that rhyme with these words.

tire   loft   late

4. Write the list words that fit the boxes.

a) If we go, ⬚⬚⬚⬚ we will see a bear.

b) I will see you ⬚⬚⬚⬚⬚ this week.

c) Do you like ⬚⬚⬚⬚⬚ puzzles?

The **-ing** gives you lots of Word Power.

Word Power

1. Add the **-ing** ending to the base words on each soccer ball.

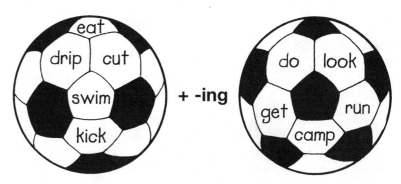

eat
drip cut
swim
kick

+ **-ing**

do look
get run
camp

2. Write an **-ing** word for each picture.

a)

b)

c)

d)

3. Solve the riddles. Write the answers in your notebook.

a) I don't mean yes
   And I don't mean no,
   I mean _____ .

b) The sun rises
   Birds sing
   It must be _____ .

4. Write sentences using the pairs of words below.

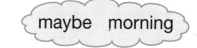

fire   camping

maybe   morning

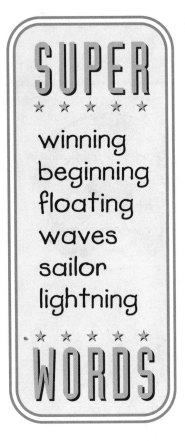

SUPER
★ ★ ★ ★ ★
winning
beginning
floating
waves
sailor
lightning
. ★ ★ ★ ★ ★
WORDS

Challenges with Words

1. Each set of words contains one Super Word. Write the Super Word in each set.

   a) saves   ways   waves   caves

   b) boating   coating   joking   floating

   c) tailor   sailor   jailer   sailing

   d) lightning   fighting   lighting   frightening

2. Complete each sentence with a Super Word.

   a) The _____ has sailed to many lands.
   b) She got a prize for _____ three races.
   c) We came late and missed the _____ of the story.
   d) The boat rocked up and down on the _____ .
   e) I saw a flash of _____ and heard the roar of thunder.
   f) _____ is easy if you wear a life jacket.

Check the dictionary for words that start with **fl**.

3. Write the words below in a list. Then write their base words next to them.

   winning   beginning   floating   rolling   racing

4. **Floating** begins with the blend **fl**. Write as many words as you can that begin with **fl**.

5. Write the opposites of these words.

   a) beginning   <u>ending</u>
   b) starting   _____
   c) floating   _____
   d) laughing   _____
   e) winning   _____
   f) going   _____

48

6. Write the meanings of these words ending in **or**.

Example

A sailor is someone who sails on a ship.

a) doctor

b) actor

c) author

7. Complete each set of words with a Super Word. Write the words in your notebook.

a) water   rolling   crashing   _____

b) ribbon   trophy   first   _____

c) uniform   ship   ocean   _____

d) crash   thunder   flash   _____

e) starting   first   early   _____

An editor is someone who checks your writing for mistakes.

8. a) Write a story using some of these Super Words.

waves   floating   sailor   lightning

b) Work with an editing partner. Use suggestions your partner makes to write a second draft of your story.

Long **e** Vowels with **r**

ea

lea**n**   **ear**

must
clean
eating
along
near
could
mean
lunch
being
year
began
would

See the Words

Look at each word in the list.

Say the Words

1. Say each word. Listen for each sound.

mean   clean   near   year

could   would   eating   being

began   lunch   must   along

2. Say the words. Listen for the vowel sounds.

ear   bean   seat

What letters spell the long **e** sound as in **me**?
What letters spell the long **e** + **r** as in **ear**?

✓ Precheck

**Check your work.
Write the words
you misspelled.**

★ Powerbooster ★

In some words, like **clean**, we use the letters **ea**
to spell the long **e** sound.

When we add **r** to long **e**, we have the sound we
hear in **ear**.

Write the Words

1. a) Read the story.

Last <u>year</u> there was a boy in our class named Max. He <u>would</u> always stand <u>near</u> the drinking fountain and spray water on everybody he <u>could</u> as they walked <u>along</u> the hall. One day while we were <u>eating</u> <u>lunch</u> he sprayed juice all over my <u>clean</u> shirt. I <u>began</u> to shout, "Max you <u>must</u> stop <u>being</u> so <u>mean</u>!"

Max was very surprised. "I was just playing a joke," he said. Then Max said he was sorry and he was never mean again.

b) Look for the list words in the story. Write them in your notebook.

2. Write the list words that have the long **e** sound as in **me**. Underline the words that spell the long **e** sound with the letters **ea**.

3. Write the two list words that fit this box.

4. Complete the sentences with list words.

a) We eat _____ at noon.
b) You _____ be careful on the road.
c) We walked _____ the creek with our dog.

Word Power

1. Write **ea** words to match these meanings.

   a) dinner or breakfast   m _ _ l
   b) comes from animals   m _ _ t
   c) a fruit with fuzz on it   p _ _ ch
   d) used to make flour   wh _ _ t
   e) a holiday meal   f _ _ _ t
   f) a person who helps you learn t _ _ ch _ _

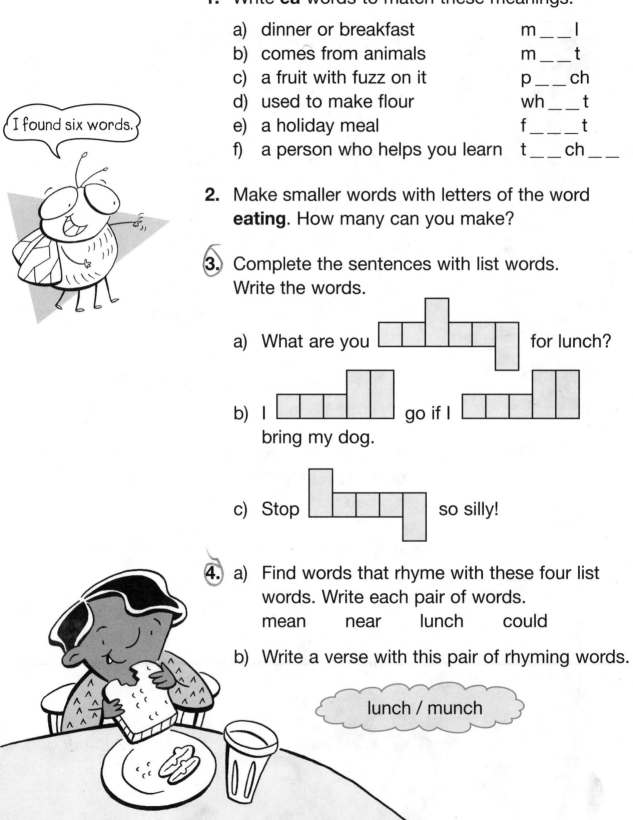

I found six words.

2. Make smaller words with letters of the word **eating**. How many can you make?

3. Complete the sentences with list words. Write the words.

   a) What are you ⬚⬚⬚⬚⬚ for lunch?

   b) I ⬚⬚⬚⬚ go if I ⬚⬚⬚⬚ bring my dog.

   c) Stop ⬚⬚⬚⬚ so silly!

4. a) Find words that rhyme with these four list words. Write each pair of words.
      mean   near   lunch   could

   b) Write a verse with this pair of rhyming words.

      lunch / munch

52

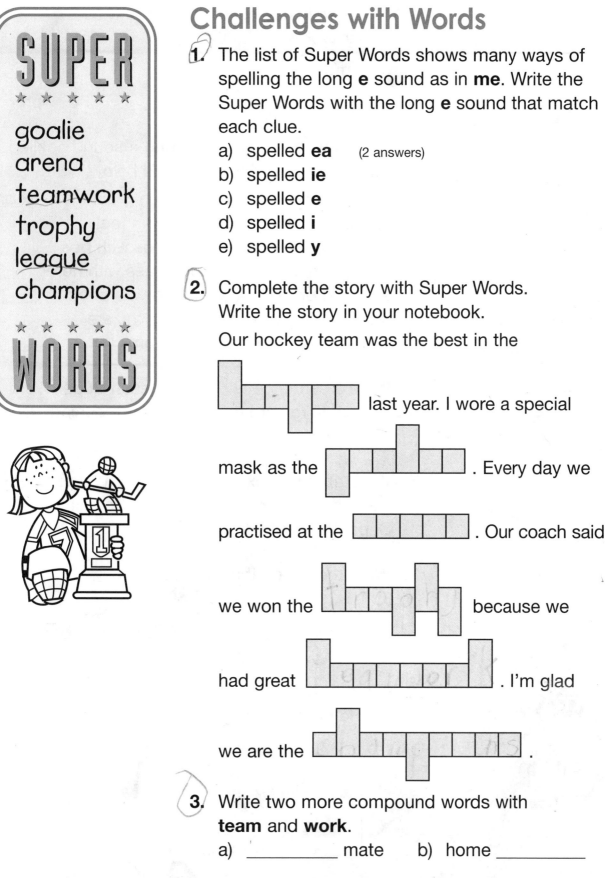

SUPER WORDS

goalie
arena
teamwork
trophy
league
champions

Challenges with Words

1. The list of Super Words shows many ways of spelling the long **e** sound as in **me**. Write the Super Words with the long **e** sound that match each clue.
   a) spelled **ea**   (2 answers)
   b) spelled **ie**
   c) spelled **e**
   d) spelled **i**
   e) spelled **y**

2. Complete the story with Super Words. Write the story in your notebook.

   Our hockey team was the best in the

   [ ] last year. I wore a special

   mask as the [ ]. Every day we

   practised at the [ ]. Our coach said

   we won the [trophy] because we

   had great [teamwork]. I'm glad

   we are the [champions].

3. Write two more compound words with **team** and **work**.
   a) _____ mate   b) home _____

4. The vowels have been left out of these Super Words. Write the complete word.

ch _ mp _ _ ns   l _ _ g _ _   _ r _ n _

t _ _ mw _ rk   g _ _ l _ _   tr _ ph _

5. Write a word that has the long **e** sound spelled **ea** and rhymes with the words below.

a) a vegetable that rhymes with **green**   <u>bean</u>

b) a sea animal that rhymes with **feel**   _____

c) a word for ocean that rhymes with **bee**   _____

d) a pointed weapon that rhymes with **here**   _____

e) a part of a bird that rhymes with **peek**   _____

f) an event you imagine when you are asleep that rhymes with **seem**   _____

6. Write a sentence telling what each Super Word means. If you are not sure of the meaning, use a dictionary.

7. Write about an exciting game that you played or watched in your favourite sport. Use all the Super Words if you can.

8. Write the words that fit the boxes.

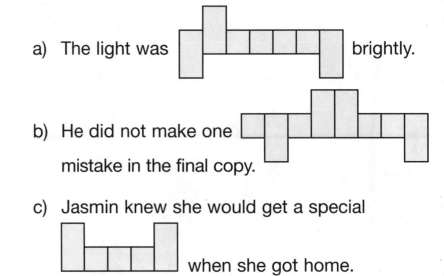

a) The light was ☐☐☐☐☐ brightly.

b) He did not make one ☐☐☐☐☐ mistake in the final copy.

c) Jasmin knew she would get a special ☐☐☐☐ when she got home.

Kids
WORDS

treat
spelling
glowing

12

STUDY STEPS

look

say

cover

write

check

Looking Back

Here is a list of words from Units 7–11 that may be hard for you.

about	first	doing	always
upon	holiday	maybe	kept
where	Saturday	could	every

1. Use the Study Steps for each word. Add some of your own review words to the list.

2. Write the words from the list below that spell the short **o** sound with the letter **a** as in **salt**.

fall	also	almost
fast	small	call
past	always	crash

3. The picture words below all have the long **e** sound as in tr**ee** and s**ea**t. Write the words.

   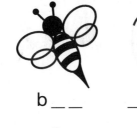    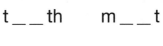

b _ _   _ _ r   f _ _ t   p _ _ ch

str _ _ m   t _ _ th   m _ _ t   qu _ _ n

Add **-ing** to each base word on the train. Write the words.

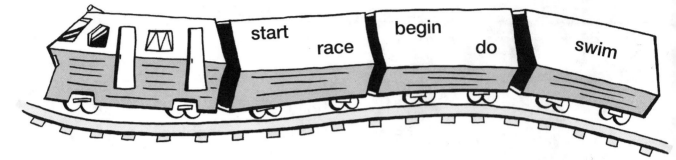

5. Complete each sentence with words from the box that have the long **a** sound spelled **ay**. Write the sentences.

stay	Saturday	days
Sunday	play	crayon

a) The best _____ of the week are _____ and _____ .

b) My parents let me _____ up late to _____ .

c) I broke my red _____ .

6. Write these words in alphabetical order.

feet	cave	fight
ate	being	doing
books	eat	dragon
clean	about	every

Don't forget! When two words start with the same letter, go to the second letter.

7. Complete each sentence with the correct word. Write the words.

a) I _____ eat breakfast in the morning.

always   already
almost   alone

b) Would you _____ me how to ski?

reach   teach
beach   peach

c) Did she _____ her new bike to school?

wide   hide
side   ride

d) They will be here by _____ o'clock.

tree   three
teeth   free

8. Choose two pages from a favourite story. Copy all the words with **-ing** endings in your notebook. Beside each of the words write the base word.

9. Now make your own review list. Find a spelling partner to dictate it to you. Use words from the Unit Tests, or words from your Personal Word List.

Winter

December holidays February icicle sled frosty slip skiing January skates hockey toboggan HOT CHOCOLATE

1. Add other **winter words** to the list above. Make a class list of winter words.

2. a) How is winter different from summer? Make four headings in your notebook like the ones below. Write words under each heading.

Summer Clothes	Winter Clothes	Summer Games	Winter Games

   b) Think of another way you could compare summer and winter. Write the headings in your notebook and fill in the spaces below them.

Summer Weather	Winter Weather

3. A magic snowflake has landed in your hand. It will grant you three wishes. Wish quickly before your snowflake melts! Write your three wishes and share them with a partner.

run

jump

Grammar Games

Verbs

A **verb** is a word we use to describe action.

1. There are a lot of great verbs that begin with **s**, and describe winter action. Write the verbs that match these pictures.

s _ i   s _ _ t _   sn _ _ b _ ard

2. Some special verbs do not describe action. The verbs in these sentences describe how someone or something **is**, **feels**, **sounds**, or **looks**.

Janet **is** cold.   The drum **sounds** loud.
She **feels** happy.   The dog **looks** sleepy.

Use the verbs from the box to complete these sentences. The picture clues will help you.

That dog _____ happy.   That cake _____ delicious.

That skunk _____ bad.   That boy _____ sick.

3. Write your own sentences with these verbs.

slide   smells   feels   looks

tastes
smells
looks
feels

Dictionary Games

1. Look at the first letter in each of the words in the picture. Write the words in alphabetical order.

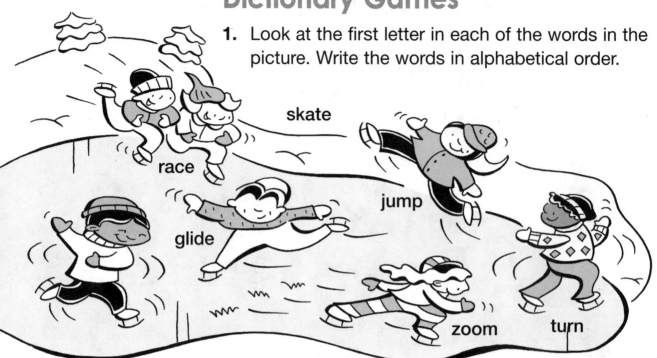

skate

race

jump

glide

zoom

turn

Proofreading

Read the story below. Find the eight words that are not spelled correctly. Talk to a partner about where the writer made a mistake. Then, rewrite the misspelled words correctly.

Danielle and Rajiv love to play outside on Saturday. They are allways the frist ones at the park. They walk down King Street untill they are inside the park gate.

"Were are all our friends?" Danielle asks. "It is allmost ten o'clock!"

"Let's put on are skates and wait for them," Rajiv says.

Danielle and Rajiv skate around the park until their freinds arrive. Then, they all go off to play togethre.

-ed Endings Vowels with **r**

call**ed** **er** socc**er**

killed
soccer
called
beach
happened
leaves
turned
supper
climbed
summer
better
team

See the Words

Look at each word in the list.

Say the Words

1. Say each word. Listen for each sound.

   killed called happened turned

   climbed beach team leaves

   summer soccer better supper

2. Say the words. Listen to the final consonant sound.

   killed called happened turned climbed

   What letters spell the consonant sound **d** at the end of the word?

3. Say the words. Listen for the sound at the end.

   summer soccer better supper

   What letters spell the sound at the end?

✓ Precheck

Check your work. Underline the parts of the words you need to study.

★ Powerbooster ★

When we write words like **killed** or **called**, the consonant sound **d** at the end is spelled **-ed**. We spell most words that have the **vowel + r** ending with **er** as in **letter** and **bigger**.

Write the Words

1. a) Read the story.

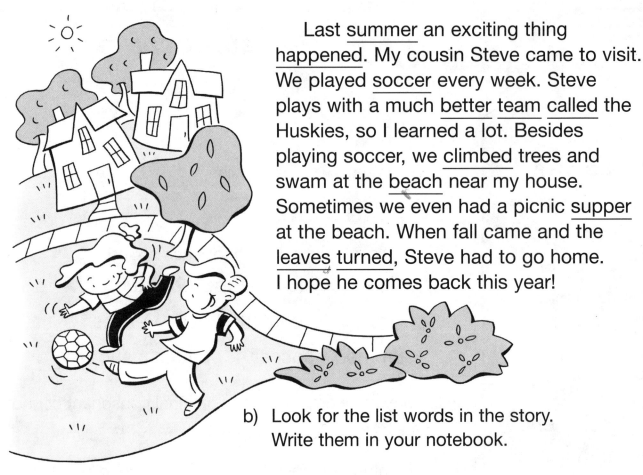

Last underline{summer} an exciting thing happened. My cousin Steve came to visit. We played soccer every week. Steve plays with a much better team called the Huskies, so I learned a lot. Besides playing soccer, we climbed trees and swam at the beach near my house. Sometimes we even had a picnic supper at the beach. When fall came and the leaves turned, Steve had to go home. I hope he comes back this year!

b) Look for the list words in the story. Write them in your notebook.

c) Write the list word that is not in the story.

k _ _ _ _ d

Notice that all the words have double consonants.

2. Write the list words that have **-ed** endings. Underline the base word for each.

3. Write the list words that have the long **e** sound spelled **ea**.

4. Write the list words that end in **er**.

Word Power

1. Add the ending **-ed** to the base words in the large box. Write the words.

-ed   spill   climb   play   fill   happen   open   glow   turn

2. Fill in the blanks with list words that have double consonants. Write the words.

_ _ ll _ _   _ _ cc _ _

_ _ ll _ _   _ _ tt _ _

_ _ pp _ _ _ _   _ _ mm _ _

These two words have something to do with water. A **beach** has water nearby. **Beach** must be the word that fits!

3. Complete each set of words with a list word. Write the word.

a) waves   swimming   _____

b) coach   players   _____

c) shouted   yelled   _____

d) branches   buds   _____

e) breakfast   lunch   _____

4. Choose two sets of words from exercise 3. Write your own sentences with some of the words in the sets.

Example   I eat **breakfast**, **lunch**, and **supper** every day.

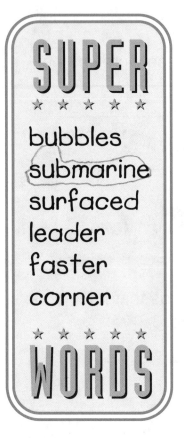

Challenges with Words

1. Complete the sentences with Super Words. Write the words in your notebook.

a) That _____ can travel under the water.

b) The _____ in the race was running _____ than everybody else.

c) We saw the _____ coming up from the divers underwater.

d) The bus stops at the _____ of the street.

e) The whale _____ in front of our boat.

2. Look at this set of words: **fast faster fastest**. Complete the sets below in the same way. Write the sets.

a) young _____ _____

b) _____ colder _____

c) _____ _____ highest

d) _____ quicker _____

e) bright _____ _____

f) _____ _____ strongest

3. Sometimes you can write a word in a way that will say something about its meaning. Look at these examples.

Write the Super Words so that they look like their meanings.

4. Unscramble the Super Words in each bubble. Write the words in your notebook.

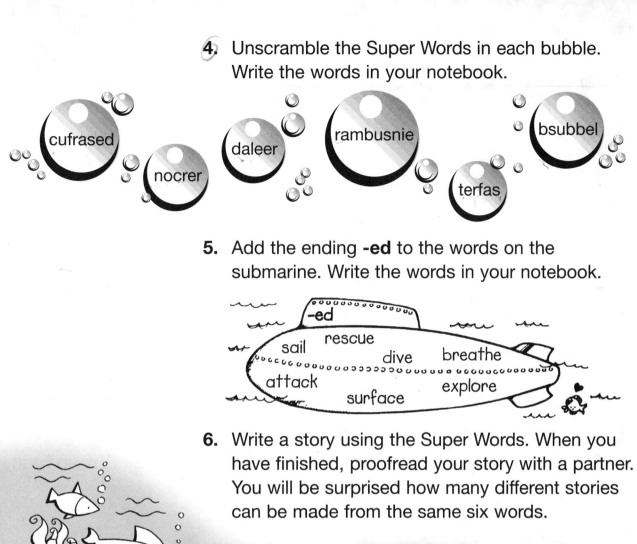

cufrased

nocrer

daleer

rambusnie

terfas

bsubbel

5. Add the ending **-ed** to the words on the submarine. Write the words in your notebook.

-ed

sail
rescue
dive
breathe
attack
surface
explore

6. Write a story using the Super Words. When you have finished, proofread your story with a partner. You will be surprised how many different stories can be made from the same six words.

Kids
WORDS

scored
pulled
chewed

7. Write the words that match the clues.

a) I rhyme with **mood**, but I have six letters.

_ _ _ w _ _

b) I have two tall letters in the middle.

_ _ l _ _ _

c) I rhyme with **bored**, and I have something to do with sports.

_ _ _ r _ _

14

Contractions
I'd

he's
I'd
died
they're
colour
couldn't
most
wouldn't
more
I'll
goes
once

✓ Precheck

Check your work. What words do you need to study?

See the Words

1. Look at each word in the list.

2. Look at the two words and the contraction.

he is — he's	I will — I'll
I would — I'd	could not —couldn't
they are — they're	would not —wouldn't

How do we show where some letters have been left out of a contraction?

Say the Words

Say each word. Listen to each sound.

I'd   I'll   died   couldn't

wouldn't   he's   they're   colour

most   goes   more   once

★ **Powerbooster** ★

We use an apostrophe ' when we write **contractions** like **I'll** or **I'd**. The apostrophe shows where one or more letters have been left out.

Write the Words

1. a) Read the story.

Every year our neighbour, Mr. Milos, <u>goes</u> to visit his sister. This year he said he <u>wouldn't</u> go because he <u>couldn't</u> leave his rose garden. <u>He's</u> very proud of his roses. <u>They're</u> the <u>most</u> beautiful <u>colour</u> you've ever seen.

"Don't worry, Mr. Milos," I told him. <u>I'll</u> give them water <u>once</u> a week, and <u>more</u> when it's hot and dry."

Mr. Milos was very glad. "I'd be sorry if my roses <u>died</u>," he said, "but I'd sure hate to miss my trip."

b) Look for the list words in the story. Write them in your notebook.

The letters of the word **one** are in **once**.

2. a) Write the list words that are contractions.
   b) Write the two words that make up each contraction.

3. Write the list word that means **one time**. Underline the letter that spells the **s** sound in this word.

4. Write the list words that fit these boxes.

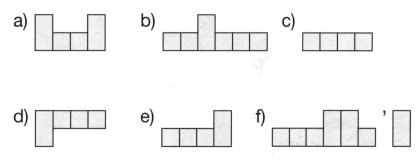

a)   b)   c)

d)   e)   f)

Word Power

1. Write contractions for the underlined words.

a) <u>He is</u> afraid that <u>I will</u> get lost.

b) <u>I would</u> be very sad if you <u>could not</u> come.

c) You <u>should not</u> touch that. <u>It is</u> dangerous!

2. Complete the sentences with the words **more** and **most**. Write the sentences.

a) The ant has _____ legs than the mouse.

b) The spider has _____ legs than the ant.

c) The spider has the _____ legs.

3. The word **colour** ends with **our**. Write the words with **our** that fit these sentences.

a) Mr. Spiros is our n o u g h b o u r.

b) His house is my f a v o u r i t e c o l o u r.

4. Write a rhyming word for each of these list words.

most   died   more   goes

5. a) Write verses using the rhyming words you wrote above.

Example   What I like most,
Is cheese on toast.

b) Read your verse to a partner.

Don't forget! Rhyming words are not always spelled the same.

66

SUPER
★ ★ ★ ★ ★
thirsty
desert
cactus
temperature
silence
weren't
★ ★ ★ ★ ★
WORDS

Challenges with Words

1. a) Fill in the blanks with Super Words.
   Write the story in your notebook.

   The lost woman wandered across the dusty
   _____ . She had not had a drink of water in
   ten hours, and was very _____ . There
   _____ any trees for shade. She sat next to
   a giant _____ with prickly arms. The
   _____ was over forty degrees, and all
   around her she heard only _____ .
   Suddenly…

   b) Now finish the story using your own ideas.

2. Write the Super Words that match these clues.

   a) a word that has four syllables

   b) a word with the sound **s** spelled with both
      s and **c**

   c) a word that has an **s** surrounded by **e**'s

   d) a word that has two **c**'s, you don't want to
      touch it

   e) a word almost like the word for the number 30

3. Write the contractions that rhyme with these
   words.

   a) cheese h _'_   d) wheel s _ _'_ _

   b) died I'_   e) time I'_

   c) while I'_ _   f) ant c _ _'_

4. How many words can you make with the letters
   in **temperature**? Try to find at least ten smaller
   words. Write your words.

5. Complete these sentences with your own words. Think carefully about your answers. Write the sentences in your notebook.

a) Being thirsty is like being hungry because _____ .
Being thirsty is different than being hungry because _____ .

b) A cactus is like a rose because _____ .
A cactus is different than a rose because _____ .

c) A desert is like a beach because _____ .
A desert is different than a beach because _____ .

6. Complete each set of words with a Super Word. Write the words.

a) fever   chills   _____

b) sand   dunes   _____

c) hungry   hot   _____

d) stillness   quiet   _____

7. Imagine you are going to explore a desert. What should you do so you won't get hurt or lost? Write a plan for your exploration.

Plans for Exploring the Desert

1. Get a good map.

2. Ask someone to go with me.

15

Compound Words
someone

someone
sure
everyone
sky
everybody
use
himself
fly
myself
try
that's
didn't

See the Words

Look at each word in the list.

Say the Words

1. Say each word. Listen for each sound.

   someone   everyone   everybody   himself

   myself   fly   try   sky

   sure   use   that's   didn't

2. Say the words. Listen for two shorter words in each long word. These long words are called **compound words**.

   someone   everyone   himself   myself

✓ Precheck

Check your work. Write the words you misspelled.

★ Powerbooster ★

It is sometimes easier to spell a **compound word** like **football** if you think of it as two shorter words **foot** + **ball**.

Write the Words

1. **a)** .Read the story.

I know <u>someone</u> in Alberta who likes to jump off mountain tops. <u>That's</u> not as strange as it sounds. She straps herself into a hang glider and floats through the <u>sky</u>. I'm <u>sure</u> I'd be afraid to <u>try</u> that <u>myself</u>. What if the glider <u>didn't</u> hold you up? What if you crashed? I guess hang gliding is not a sport for <u>everyone</u>. I think I'll <u>use</u> a plane to <u>fly</u> when I grow up, like <u>everybody</u> else.

b) Look for the list words in the story. Write them in your notebook.

c) Write the list word that is not in the story.

h <u>i m s e l</u> f

2. Write the compound words in the list. Put boxes around the two smaller words in each compound.

3. Write the list words that are contractions.

4. Write the list word that has the sound **sh** spelled with the letter **s**.

5. Write the list words that fit the blanks.

a) I'd like to <u>f _ _</u> in the <u>s _ _ _</u> .

b) Be <u>s _ _ _ _</u> to <u>t _ _</u> your best.

c) <u>T _ _ _ _'_</u> not the way to <u>u _ _</u> scissors.

70

Word Power

1. Write these sentences using the word and picture clues.

   a) Some + one took my 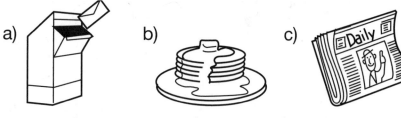 .

   b) Every + body went to the + .

   c) Didn't U give a + to every + one ?

I have a mailbox beside my front door.

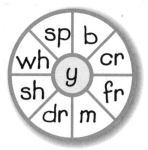

2. Write the compound word for each clue.

   a)   b)   c)

3. Join the letters on the outside circle with the letter **y** to write words that rhyme with **try**.

   sp b
   wh cr
   y
   sh fr
   dr m

4. Write a sentence that uses three of the words you made in exercise 3.

   Example   Why did my friend start to cry?

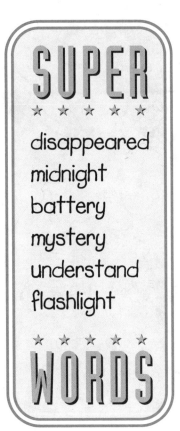

SUPER
★ ★ ★ ★ ★
disappeared
midnight
battery
mystery
understand
flashlight
★ ★ ★ ★ ★
WORDS

Challenges with Words

1. Be a word detective. Use these clues to discover Super Words. Write the words.

   a) two words that have the long **i** spelled **igh**

   b) two words with double consonants

   c) a word containing two **y**'s

   d) a word that means 'to get the meaning of'

2. Solve the riddles with Super Words. Write the words.

   a) The clock strikes twelve
      But it is not noon.
      It must be _____.

   b) When it's dark and scary
      I'll show you the way.
      I am a _____.

3. Complete the Super Words on each magnifying glass.

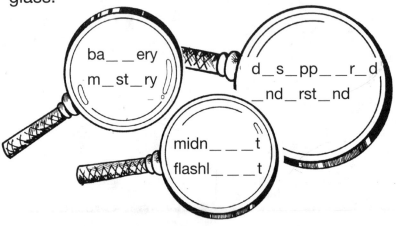

ba_ _ery
m_st_ry

d_s_pp_ _r_d
_nd_rst_nd

midn_ _ _ _t
flashl_ _ _ _t

4. Three of the Super Words are compound words. Write another compound with each of the underlined words.

   a) <u>under</u>stand   b) flash<u>light</u>   c) mid<u>night</u>

I dislike mosquitoes.

5. The prefix **dis-** usually makes a word mean the opposite. Match the words in list A with the meanings in list B. Write the words and meanings in your notebook.

	A	B
a)	disagree	to not follow the rules
b)	dishonest	to have a bad feeling
c)	dislike	to have an opposite idea
d)	disobey	not to be trusted

6. Now complete these sentences with the words in exercise 5. Write the sentences.

a) I dis_____ getting my feet wet.

b) If you tell a lie, you are being dis_____ .

c) Never dis_____ the school crossing guard.

d) I dis_____ with your answer.

7. Write your own mystery story! Fill in the blanks with your ideas. Then write about what happens next.

One night while I was visiting _____ , I heard a _____ and saw _____ . I grabbed the flashlight by my bed and went carefully _____ . The clock in the _____ struck midnight. Suddenly, the battery on my flashlight went dead, and I…

8. Write the words that fit the sentences below.

a) Always stop at a *stoplight*.

b) I *cannot* get the lid off this jar!

c) My favourite game is _____.

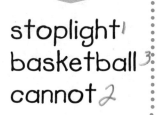

Kids WORDS

stoplight¹
basketball³
cannot²

73

16

Vowels with **r**

ar

st**ar**s

anything
far
everything
cars
afternoon
stars
baseball
sharp
sharks
any
toy
were

See the Words

Look at each word in the list.

Say the Words

1. Say each word. Listen for each sound.

   anything   everything   far   cars

   stars   sharp   sharks   any

   were   toy   afternoon   baseball

2. Say the words. Listen for the vowel sounds.

   cars   stars   sharks

What letters spell the **ar** sound as in **far**?

★ **Powerbooster** ★

We use the letters **ar** to spell the **ar** sound as in **far** and **sharp**.

74

Write the Words

1. a) Read the story.

It was Saturday afternoon. I couldn't go and play baseball until my room was clean. It was far from tidy! Everything was on the floor. There wasn't anything on the shelves. All my toy cars were under my bed.

But the worst part of the job was cleaning my shark aquarium. Even small sharks have sharp teeth! "I'll be working here until the stars come out," I sighed. "I won't have any time to play ball."

b) Look for the list words in the story. Write them in your notebook.

2. Write the list words that have the **ar** sound as in **far**.

3. Write the three list words that mean **more than one**. Circle the letter that shows **more than one**.

4. Write the list words that are compound words.

5. Find the list words that fit the boxes. Write the sentences.

a) We ☐☐☐☐ playing ☐☐☐☐☐☐☐☐ .

b) Do you have ☐☐☐ ☐☐☐ cars?

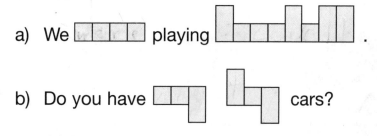

Word Power

1. Unscramble the words in these sentences. Write the words.

   a) The teeth on the `hrasks` are very `prahs` .

   b) There `erwe` many `rasc` on the road.

   c) Can you see `yna` `atssr` tonight?

2. Use words from each list to write as many compound words as you can.

A	B
some	thing
every	one
any	body

3. Change the first letter of **dark** and **dart** to make new words.

   a) **dark**   m _ _ _   p _ _ _ _   b _ _ _ _   l _ _ _ _

   b) **dart**   c _ _ _ _   p _ _ _ _   st _ _ _ _   t _ _ _ _

4. a) Solve the riddle. Write the list word.
I come after morning
And before night.
What am I? _____

   b) Write your own riddles for two of these words.

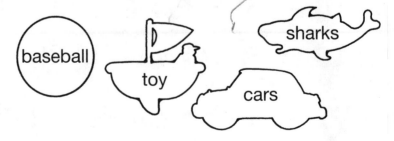

baseball   toy   sharks   cars

   c) Try your riddles on a partner.

Why did the s_ _ _ _ _ _ brush their teeth? Because they wanted to look s_ _ _ _ _!

SUPER

★ ★ ★ ★ ★

anywhere
farther
blood
nurse
ambulance
medicine

★ ★ ★ ★ ★

WORDS

Challenges with Words

1. Write the Super Words in alphabetical order.

2. Write the Super Words that fit the clues.

  a) a vehicle for taking
       people to the hospital _ _ _ _ _ _ _ _ _ _

  b) used for treating illness _ _ _ _ _ _ _ _ _

  c) any place at all _ _ _ _ _ _ _ _ _

  d) a greater distance _ _ _ _ _ _ _ _

  e) carries oxygen through the body _ _ _ _ _ _

  f) a person who helps sick people _ _ _ _ _ _

3. Complete these sentences with Super Words. Write the sentences.

  a) After the accident, the _____ took the child to the hospital.

  b) Your heart pumps _____ to the rest of your body.

  c) The _____ gave the child some _____ .

  d) You may go _____ you wish.

  e) Robin can run _____ than I can.

4. Write your own fill-in-the-blank sentences with the Super Words. Trade your sentences with a partner.

5. Write the opposites of these words. They all have the **ar** sound as in **car**.

  a) smaller   l a r g e r

  b) easier   h _ _ d _ _

  c) nearer   f _ _ t _ _ _ _

  d) stopped   s _ _ _ t _ _

77

6. What would you do in these emergencies? Write a sentence for each one. Use as many Super Words as you can.

a) You are alone at home when a fire breaks out.

b) Your friend falls off his bike and can't move his leg.

c) You think your little sister has swallowed some poison.

d) Your friend cuts her foot badly while you are swimming at the beach.

7. Imagine you work helping people or animals that are sick or hurt.

a) Write a short paragraph about a day at work. Proofread your paragraph with a partner.

b) Draw a picture of yourself at work.

17

Long **o**   **-ed** Endings
oa
r**oa**d   jump**ed**

---

road
jumped
helped
coat
wished
should
ship
boat
picked
asked
afraid
its

See the Words

Look at each word in the list.

Say the Words

1. Say each word. Listen for each sound.

   helped   picked   wished   asked

   jumped   its   boat   coat

   road   should   ship   afraid

2. Say the words. Listen for the vowel sounds.

   boat   coat   soap

   What letters spell the long **o** sound as in **open**?

3. Say the words. Listen for the final consonant sound.

   helped   wished   picked   jumped

   What letters spell the consonant sound **t**?

✔ Precheck

Check your work. Write the words you misspelled.

★ Powerbooster ★

In some words we spell the long **o** sound with the letters **oa**, as in **boat** and **coat**.

When we write words like **jumped** or **helped**, we spell the sound **t** with **-ed**.

79

Write the Words

1. a) Read the story.

One day I <u>asked</u> my Aunt Janet to take me out on her fishing <u>boat</u>. It's as big as a small <u>ship</u>. We walked down the <u>road</u> to the dock and <u>jumped</u> aboard. "You <u>should</u> put on a <u>coat</u>," said Aunt Janet. "Looks like a storm coming." She <u>picked</u> up the yellow raincoat and <u>helped</u> me put it on. I did up <u>its</u> hood tight. When the storm hit, I was a <u>bit</u> afraid. I <u>wished</u> the waves wouldn't rock the boat. But Aunt Janet is a good sailor, and soon we were safely home.

b) Look for the list words in the story. Write them in your notebook.

2. Write the list words that have -**ed** endings. Underline the base word for each.

3. Write the list words that have the long **o** sound as in **open**. Underline the letters that spell the long **o**.

4. Write the list words that fit the boxes.

a)  b) c)

5. Write the list word that rhymes with **sits**.

Word Power

1. Look at the pictures. They all have the long **o** sound spelled **oa**. Write the words.

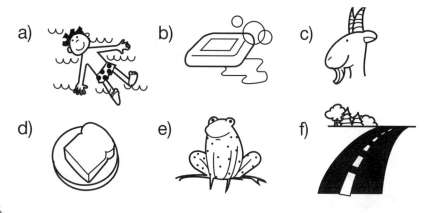

a)   b)   c)

d)   e)   f)

Hint! **It's** is a contraction for **it is**, but **its** means 'belonging to it!'

2. The words **it's** and **its** sound the same, but they have different meanings and spellings.
Complete these sentences with **it's** and **its**.
Write the sentences.

a) _____ a puppy. It has finished _____ dinner.

b) _____ a perfect day for fishing.

c) The robin is teaching _____ babies to fly.

3. Use the base words and the endings to write as many words as you can.

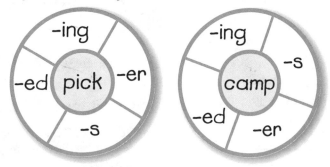

4. a) Choose two words from exercise 3.
Write a sentence with each word.

b) Paint or draw an illustration for one of your sentences.

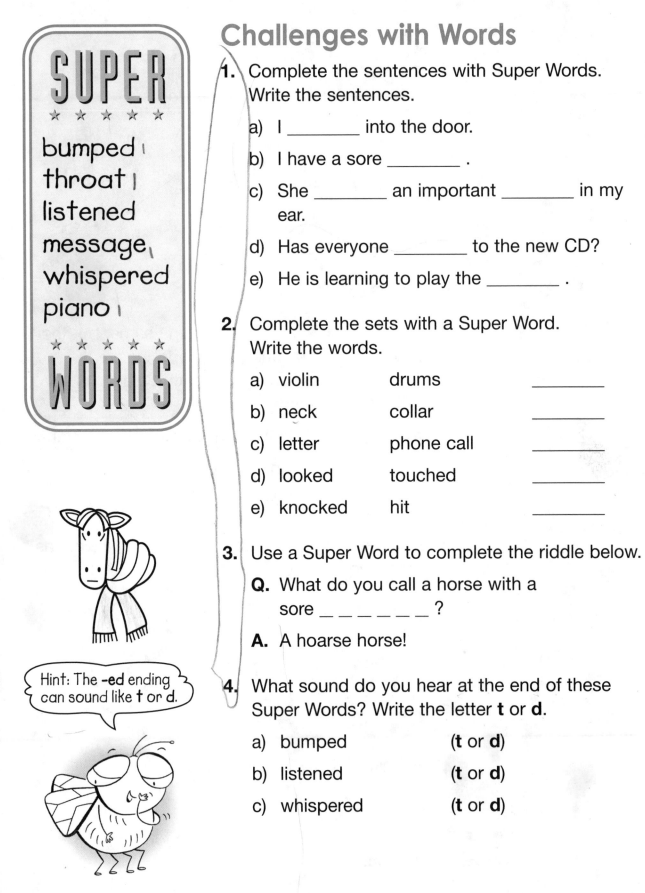

Challenges with Words

SUPER
★ ★ ★ ★ ★
bumped
throat
listened
message
whispered
piano
★ ★ ★ ★ ★
WORDS

1. Complete the sentences with Super Words. Write the sentences.

   a) I _____ into the door.

   b) I have a sore _____ .

   c) She _____ an important _____ in my ear.

   d) Has everyone _____ to the new CD?

   e) He is learning to play the _____ .

2. Complete the sets with a Super Word. Write the words.

   a) violin   drums   _____

   b) neck   collar   _____

   c) letter   phone call   _____

   d) looked   touched   _____

   e) knocked   hit   _____

3. Use a Super Word to complete the riddle below.

   Q. What do you call a horse with a sore _ _ _ _ _ _ ?

   A. A hoarse horse!

Hint: The **-ed** ending can sound like **t** or **d**.

4. What sound do you hear at the end of these Super Words? Write the letter **t** or **d**.

   a) bumped   (**t** or **d**)

   b) listened   (**t** or **d**)

   c) whispered   (**t** or **d**)

5. Find words that fit the blanks. Use only the letters of the word **listened**. Write the words.

a) something you use to catch fish   _ _ _

b) you make a shopping _____   _ _ _ _

c) a place where an animal lives   _ _ _ _

d) something made with a pencil and ruler   _ _ _ _

e) more than nine but less than eleven   _ _ _ _

f) you _____ a letter or a package   _ _ _ _

6. Complete the sentences in this story using the **-ed** form of the words in brackets and words of your own. The first one is done for you. Finish the story in your own words.

a) I got a message that Sam had called me at three o'clock. (call)

b) When I got the message, I _____ (phone) Sam back.

c) A voice _____ (whisper) in my ear that _____.

d) I listened and then I _____ (race) _____.

e) I _____ (open) Sam's door and _____ (dash) into Sam's living room.

f) I _____ (notice)...

7. Unscramble the words to complete the sentences.

a) The big dog dpopep up from behind the chair.

b) In the rkda I wasn't sure what it was.

c) You should have heard Sam oman when he saw the mess!

Kids
WORDS

dark
popped
moan

Looking Back

Here is a list of words from Units 13–17 that may be hard for you.

happened	goes	should	colour
climbed	were	afraid	sure
once	fly	they're	coat

STUDY STEPS

1. Follow the Study Steps for each word. Add some words from your Personal Word List.

2. Use **ar** to complete the following words. Write the words in your notebook.

c _ _   d _ _ ts

b _ _ ns   st _ _ _ _ s

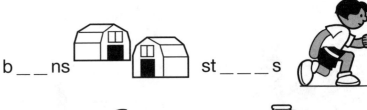

sh _ _ ks   h _ _ p

3. Remember that we add -**s** to most words when we want to show the plural or **more than one**. Write the plurals of these words.

week	team es	boat	star
cave	hill	trip	girl
shark	coat	duck	egg
game	snake	friend	ghost

4. Join the base words in lists A and B to make compound words. Write them in your notebook.

A	B
every	ball
him	noon
some	one
any	self
base	body
after	thing

5. Choose a word to fit each sentence. Write the words.

a) I lost a button off my _____ .

coat	moat
goat	float

b) For breakfast I like to eat _____ .

roast	coast
boast	toast

c) Would you like to sail in my _____ ?

float	coat
boat	oat

6. Write contractions for the underlined words.

a) I <u>could not</u> come yesterday because the car <u>would not</u> start.

b) <u>I will</u> see if he is here.

c) <u>They are</u> so happy <u>she is</u> feeling better.

d) <u>We will</u> help you find your book.

e) <u>I am</u> sorry. I <u>did not</u> mean to hurt you.

f) <u>We are</u> glad she <u>is not</u> angry.

7. Add -**ed** to these base words. Write the words.

clean   spill   jump   crash

happen   play   walk   whisper

Hint! These words end in **er** or **or**.

8. Write the word for each picture. All the spaces will have a **vowel + r**.

a) farm __ __   b) tig __ __   c) visit __ __

d) doct __ __   e) runn __ __   f) conduct __ __

9. Divide a page in your notebook into two columns. Write the headings **er** and **or** at the top of each column. Look through a book to find ten words that have the endings **er** or **or**.

10. Now make your own review list.
Use words from your Personal Word List, Super Words, or problem words from the Unit Tests.

Find a partner to dictate your words to you.

Dinosaurs

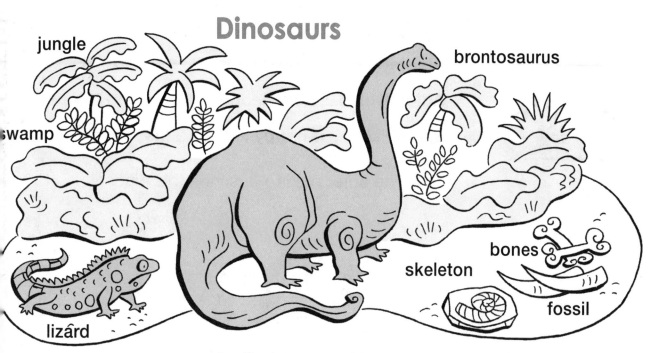

jungle

swamp

brontosaurus

skeleton

bones

fossil

lizârd

1. Brainstorm with your classmates about dinosaurs. Make a list of dinosaur words to use in your writing.

2. You step into a time machine and are sent back 200 million years! As you step out of the time machine, you come face to face with tyrannosaurus rex, one of the largest dinosaurs that ever lived. Write about what happens next.

3. Describe the prehistoric land you find yourself in. What do you see? What can you smell and hear?

Grammar Games

Adjectives tell about nouns.

Adjectives describe **people**, **places**, and **things**.

a **red** bike   a **happy** kid   a **fast** ride

1. Write adjectives to describe this dinosaur.

   a) This dinosaur is very (strong/weak).

   b) It is (fast/slow).

   c) It is (heavy/light).

   d) It is (huge/small).

2. Complete these sentences with colour adjectives that describe you and your clothes. Write the sentences in your notebook.

   I have _____ hair.

   I have_____ eyes.

   I have_____ socks.

   I have_____ shoes.

3. **Adjectives** usually come before a noun. Write these sentences in the correct order.

   a) dinosaurs lived Huge ago. long

   b) laid dinosaurs eggs. Some

   c) had Meat-eaters teeth. big

Dictionary Games

Alphabetical Order

When two words begin with the same letter, like
dinosaur and **down**, we have to look at the second
letter to put them in alphabetical order.

Dinosaur comes before **down**, because **di** comes
before **do**.

1. Write these pairs of words in alphabetical order.

swamp	skeleton	1._____	2._____
far	fossil	1._____	2._____
lake	lizard	1._____	2._____
bones	back	1._____	2._____
teeth	tail	1._____	2._____

2. Write these dinosaur names in alphabetical
order. Look at the second letter if two names
begin with the same letter.

brontosaurus	1._____
stegosaurus	2._____
tyrannosaurus	3._____
triceratops	4._____
ankylosaurus	5._____

19

-ed Endings   Long **i**

igh

want**ed**   **l**igh**t**

---

wanted ✓
light ✓
started ✓
night ✓
decided ✓
fight ✓
haunted ✓
right ✓
few ✓
many ✓
kind ✓
plant ✓

See the Words

Look at each word in the list.

Say the Words

1. Say each word. Listen for each sound.

   wanted   started   decided   haunted

   light   night   fight   right

   few   many   kind   plant

2. Say the words. Listen to the final syllable.

   wanted   started   haunted   decided

   How is **-ed** pronounced in these words?

3. Say the words. Listen to the vowel sounds.

   light   night   fight   right

   What letters spell the long **i** sound as in **ice**?

✓ Precheck

Check your work. What words do you need to study?

★ Powerbooster ★

In some words the **-ed** ending is pronounced as a separate syllable.

In some words we spell the long **i** sound with the letters **igh** as in **fight** and **right**.

Write the Words

1. a) Read the story.

There was a <u>haunted</u> house <u>right</u> on Vito's and Tina's street. They liked to explore it. One <u>night</u> as they <u>started</u> up the front path, they saw a long green arm waving in the <u>light</u> of the window. Then they saw another green arm, and another. Vito suddenly <u>wanted</u> to go home. "I could <u>fight</u> a <u>few</u> ghosts, but that's too <u>many</u>," he <u>decided</u>.

"Vito, it's just some <u>kind</u> of <u>plant</u> in the window," laughed Tina, but Vito was gone.

b) Look for the list words in the story. Write them in your notebook.

2. Write the four list words that have an **-ed** ending.

3. Write the six list words that have the long **i** sound as in **ice**. Underline the letters that spell the long **i**.

4. Write the two list words that are opposites.

5. Write the two list words that begin with a consonant blend.

Pl and **st** are **blends** because two sounds are blended together.

Kind has two meanings.

Word Power

1. Complete the sentences with list words.
   Write the words.
   a) Yesterday there were only a <u>f</u> _ _ bees, but today there are <u>m</u> _ <u>n</u> _ .
   b) You were very <u>k</u> _ _ _ to help me last <u>n</u> _ _ _ <u>t</u> .
   c) We <u>w</u> _ _ <u>t</u> _ _ to stay away from the <u>h</u> _ _ <u>n</u> <u>t</u> _ <u>d</u> house.
   d) A <u>p</u> _ _ _ <u>t</u> needs water and <u>l</u> _ _ _ <u>t</u> to grow.

2. Add the letters on the points of the star to **ight**. Write these words that rhyme with **light** in your notebook.

3. Complete the sentences with the words you made in exercise 2. Write the sentences.
   a) The stars shine at _____ .
   b) My shoes are too _____ .
   c) Is this answer _____ or wrong?
   d) I _____ go to the show tonight.
   e) The rainbow was a beautiful _____ .

4. Add **-ed** to these base words. Write the words.

   want   lift   plant   wait   need

5. a) Finish this story with your own words.

   > The door squeaked open. The room was dark. Suddenly _____.

   b) Read your story to a partner.

SUPER

★ ★ ★ ★ ★

sounded
interested
loaded
agreed
strong
delighted

★ ★ ★ ★ ★

WORDS

b	c	j	f	a	l
m	t	a	k	g	n
i	q	h	e	r	v
o	d	s	u	e	y
l	o	a	d	e	d
p	w	g	r	d	x

Challenges with Words

1. Use the Super Words to fill in the blanks. Write the sentences.

   a) My aunt ☐☐☐☐☐☐ happy on the telephone.

   b) A ☐☐☐☐☐ person ☐☐☐☐☐ our furniture on a truck.

   c) Karen was ☐☐☐☐☐☐☐ when she won.

   d) Sean ☐☐☐☐☐ to help me.

   e) I'm ☐☐☐☐☐☐☐ in everything!

2. Make a word search with your Super Words and other words. Trade it with a friend.

3. Write a sentence that tells the meaning of the underlined word in each sentence. Look at the base word for a clue.

   a) The airplane was <u>grounded</u> because of fog.

   b) The explorers <u>rounded</u> the tip of South America.

4. Use the clues to complete the puzzle with words that rhyme with **strong**. Write the words.

   a) opposite of short   _ ong

   b) opposite of right   _ _ ong

   c) something to sing   _ ong

   d) to be the property of   _ _ _ ong

5. Write opposites for these Super Words.

interested   strong   agreed   loaded

6. Write words that match the clues. They all have the long **i** sound spelled **igh**.

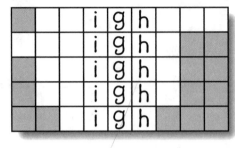

a) make afraid
b) make happy
c) very shiny
d) a trip through the air
e) a sad sound

7. When two people have the same opinion about something, they **agree**. When they have different opinions, they **disagree**. Write a statement that your classmates will agree or disagree with.

Ask them for their reasons. Then fill in a chart like the one below.

Kids should be able to watch the TV programs they choose	
Agreed	Disagreed
Dana – Kids know what they like.	Randy – Some TV programs are on too late at night.

Kids
WORDS

printed
acted
sigh

8. Write the words that fit the shapes below.

a) Maria [   ] her name on her picture.

b) She gave a big [   ], she was so happy.

c) She [   ] as if she had been working on her picture for hours.

20

Base Words and Endings

-ed
lov**ed**

loved ✓
does ✓
scared ✓
those ✓
wagged ✓
than ✓
stopped ✓
window ✓
yellow ✓
wear ✓
tail ✓
only ✓

See the Words

1. Look at each word in the list.

2. Look at the words. Notice the base word for each one.

   loved   scared   tired

   What happens when you add **-ed** to a word ending in **e**?

3. Look at the words. Notice the base word for each one.

   stopped   hummed   wagged

   What happens when you add **-ed** to a word ending in one vowel plus one consonant?

Say the Words

Say each word. Listen to each sound.

loved   scared   wagged   stopped

those   than   window   yellow

wear   tail   only   does

✓ Precheck

Check your work. What words do you need to study?

★ Powerbooster ★

When you add **-ed** to a word ending in **e**, drop one **e**. When you add **-ed** to a word ending in one vowel plus one consonant, double the consonant.

Write the Words

1. a) Read the story.

Jerry <u>loved</u> dogs. One day he <u>stopped</u> to watch three <u>yellow</u> pups in the pet shop <u>window</u>. "How much <u>does</u> one of <u>those</u> pups cost?" he asked.

They cost more <u>than</u> Jerry had. His dad said he could sweep the garage to earn money. He got so tired he thought his arms would <u>wear</u> out, but at last he had enough money. He rushed to the pet shop. <u>Only</u> one pup was left. When Jerry picked it up it wasn't <u>scared</u>. It just <u>wagged</u> its <u>tail</u>.

"I'm going to call you 'Sweeper,'" Jerry said, and he took the pup home.

b) Look for the list words in the story. Write them in your notebook.

2. Write the four list words that end in **-ed**.

3. Write the two list words that have the long **o** sound as in **open** spelled **ow**.

4. Fill in the boxes with list words. Write the sentence.

I think ☐☐☐☐ girls are taller ☐☐☐

I am.

5. Write the list words that rhyme with these words.

was   hair   nail   lonely

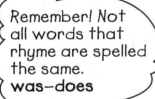

Remember! Not all words that rhyme are spelled the same.
was–does

Word Power

1. Unscramble the list word on each window.
Write the words.

e	s
o	d

h	a
n	t

r	w
e	a

y	n
o	l

2. Complete the sentences with list words.
Write the words.

a) We s _ _ _ _ _ _ d to look at the parrots in
the pet shop w _ _ d _ _ _ .

b) The dog w _ _ _ _ _ d its tail.

c) My sister d _ _ _ s not like to w _ _ r shoes.

d) When we saw the lion's t _ _ _ l we were
s _ _ _ r _ _ _ .

3. Add **-ed** to each base word. Write the words.

bake   want   fix   tug   skip

drag   touch   rub   slam   phone

4. a) Complete the story sentences with the **-ed**
form of the words in boxes.

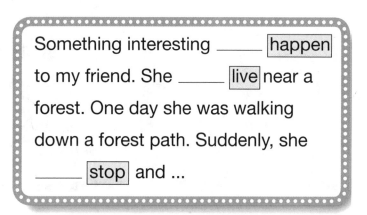

Something interesting _____ happen
to my friend. She _____ live near a
forest. One day she was walking
down a forest path. Suddenly, she
_____ stop and ...

b) Finish the story with your own ideas.

Challenges with Words

SUPER

★ ★ ★ ★ ★

captain
anchor
rescued ✓
wreck ✓
hurricane ✓
sailed ✓

★ ★ ★ ★ ★

WORDS

1. Complete each set of words with Super Words. Write the words.

a)	helped	saved	_____
b)	destroy	ruin	_____
c)	tornado	storm	_____
d)	travelled	drifted	_____
e)	crew	officer	_____
f)	chain	hook	_____

2. Solve the puzzle with Super Words. Use the clues below to help you. Write the words.

					C						
					C						
					C						
					C						
					C						

a) a bad storm with strong winds
b) the person in charge of a ship
c) saved from danger
d) is used to keep ships from floating away
e) a ship lying at the bottom of the sea

3. Add **-ed** to these words and write the words.

shove   blaze   drop   fire   save   trap

4. a) Use three of the words in question 3 to write sentences.

b) Choose one of your sentences to illustrate.

Adam

Beverly

Carlos

5. Each year hurricanes form in the Atlantic Ocean. They are named in alphabetical order after men and women. For example, Hurricane Adam, Hurricane Beverley, Hurricane Carlos. Write girls' names and boys' names for the hurricanes until you have reached the letter L.

6. The consonants have been left out of these Super Words. Put in the consonants and write the words.

a) _ u _ _ i _ a _ e   b) _ a _ _ ai _

c) _ e _ _ ue _   d) _ ai _ e _

e) _ _ e _ _   f) a _ _ _ o _

7. Write the same words with the vowels missing. Is it easier to read words when the vowels or the consonants are missing?

8. You are diving in the ocean. Suddenly you spot an old wreck.

a) Work with a partner to list some of the things you might find in the wreck.

b) When you get back on board your ship, write a letter home describing what you saw and what you found.

21

Short **o**
ough
th**ough**t

thought√
cut√
gone√
finished√
broke√
machine
brought
been
bought
kiss
done
hurt

See the Words

Look at each word in the list.

Say the Words

1. Say each word. Listen to each sound.

thought bought brought gone

finished kiss cut done

been broke machine hurt

2. Say the words. Listen for the vowel sounds.

thought bought brought

What letters spell the short **o** sound as in **hot**?

✓ Precheck

Check your work. Write the words you misspelled.

★ Powerbooster ★

A few words use the letters **ough** to spell the short **o** sound as in **brought** and **thought**.

Write the Words

1. a) Read the story.

   When we <u>finished</u> painting the house, my parents <u>bought</u> me a new bike. They said I'd <u>been</u> a big help. I was so happy, I jumped on my bike and was <u>gone</u>!

   Two blocks from home I fell and <u>broke</u> my front wheel. I also <u>hurt</u> my arm and <u>cut</u> my knee. Sadly I <u>brought</u> my bike home. "Look what I've <u>done</u>," I cried. "I've wrecked my new bike!"

   My dad gave me a <u>kiss</u>. He said he <u>thought</u> a bike repair shop would have a special <u>machine</u> to fix my front wheel.

   b) Look for the list words in the story. Write them in your notebook.

2. Write the three list words that have the short **o** sound as in **hot** spelled **ough**.

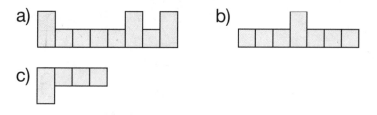

Watch for rhyming words with different spellings!
lawn - gone

3. Write list words that rhyme with each word below.

   joke   shot   skirt   fun   queen   lawn

4. Write the list words that fit these boxes.

   a) ▯▯▯▯▯▯▯   b) ▯▯▯▯▯▯

   c) ▯▯▯▯

5. Write the two list words that begin with the sound **k**. Underline the letters that spell the sound **k**.

Word Power

1. Complete this story with list words. Write them in your notebook.

What a day I've had! First, Dad sent me to the store to buy milk, but I _____ juice instead. When I _____ it home, Dad sent me back for the milk. On the way home I slipped on some ice and _____ the bag of milk. I'll be glad when today is _____ !

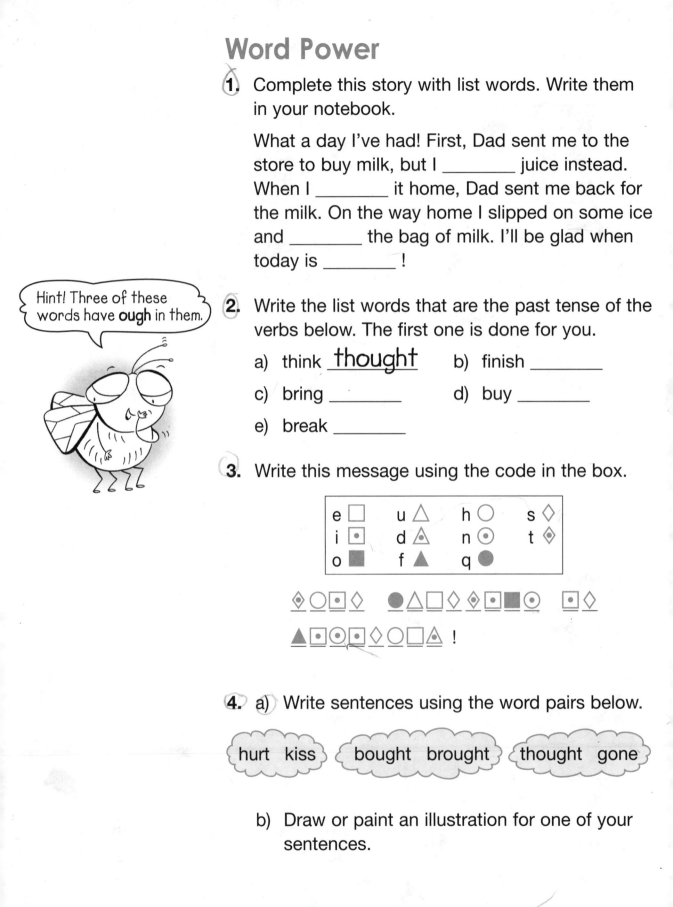

Hint! Three of these words have **ough** in them.

2. Write the list words that are the past tense of the verbs below. The first one is done for you.

a) think <u>thought</u>   b) finish _____

c) bring _____   d) buy _____

e) break _____

3. Write this message using the code in the box.

e □	u △	h ○	s ◇
i ▫	d ◭	n ⊙	t ◈
o ■	f ▲	q ●	

◈○▫◇ ●△□◇◈■▫■⊙ ▫◇
▲▫⊙▫◇○□△ !

4. a) Write sentences using the word pairs below.

hurt   kiss   bought   brought   thought   gone

b) Draw or paint an illustration for one of your sentences.

SUPER

★ ★ ★ ★ ★

fought
daughter
taught
cough
naughty
narrow

★ ★ ★ ★ ★

WORDS

Challenges with Words

1. Write the Super Words that have the short **o** sound as in **hot**. Put a triangle beside those that spell short **o** with the letters **augh**.

2. Complete the puzzle with Super Words. Use the clues to help you. Write the words.

   a) what your teacher did _ _ _ gh _
   b) disobeyed rules _ _ _ gh _ _
   c) had a battle _ _ _ gh _
   d) female child _ _ _ gh _ _ _
   e) what you do when you _ _ _ gh
   have a cold

3. Use the correct Super Word to complete the sentences. Write the words.

   a) The name of their _____ is Carmen.
   b) The children learned what their teacher _____ .
   c) The bridge is too _____ for cars to pass.
   d) You should take some _____ medicine.
   e) The children were sent to their rooms for being _____ .
   f) The two dogs _____ over the bone.

4. Make your own fill-in-the-blank sentences with the Super Words. Trade them with a partner.

5. Using only the letters in the word **daughter**, write a word to go with each meaning.

   a) the organ that pumps blood in your body h _ _ _ t
   b) to collect things together g _ _ _ _ _ r
   c) the opposite of life d _ _ _ h
   d) to exchange one thing for another t _ _ _ _ e

6. Combine word parts from the three boxes. Write as many words as you can.

Example

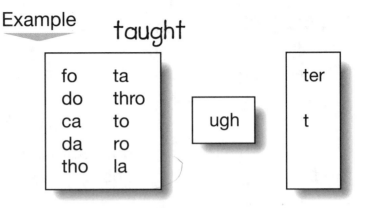

taught

fo	ta
do	thro
ca	to
da	ro
tho	la

| ugh |

| ter |
| t |

7. a) Finish the story below using as many Super Words as you can.

Twiki the mouse lived in the walls of a big house with her parents and sisters. One day, Twiki crept out of the mouse hole into the big house and…

b) Write a story beginning. Have a partner suggest events that could happen in the story. Write and illustrate it as a team.

smiled
grinned
giggled

8. Write the words that fit the clues.

a) laughed in a happy way _____

b) turned up the corners of the mouth _____

c) stretched a smile as wide as it could go _____

22

Possessives Long **o**

's   **o _ e**

dog**'s**   n**ose**

kitten's
nose
mother's
bone
dog's
hole
friend's
again
woke
around
together
another

See the Words

1. Look at each word in the list.

2. Look at the words.

mother's   dog's   friend's   kitten's

The ending **'s** means **belonging to**.
Example

The **dog's tail** means 'the tail belonging to the dog'.

Say the Words

1. Say each word. Listen for each sound.

mother's   dog's   friend's   kitten's

bone   hole   nose   woke

again   around   another   together

2. Say the words. Listen for the vowel sounds.
nose   bone   hole   woke
What letters spell the long **o** sound as in **open**?

✓ Precheck

**Check your work.
What words do you
need to study?**

★ Powerbooster ★

We use the ending **'s** to show that something belongs,
as in **mother's** and **dog's**.

The long **o** sound as in **open** is sometimes spelled o _ e.

Write the Words

1. a) Read the story.

This morning I <u>woke</u> up early with my <u>dog's</u> cold <u>nose</u> in my face. "What's the matter, Sam," I said. "Do you want to go outside?" <u>Together</u> we went downstairs. Sam sniffed <u>around</u> the <u>kitten's</u> dish as if he was trying to find something.

We went outside. Sam had been digging <u>again</u>. There was <u>another hole</u> in my <u>mother's</u> favourite flower bed. Sam started to dig. At the bottom of the hole he found his toy <u>bone</u>.

b) Look for the list words in the story.
Write them in your notebook.

c) Write the list word that is not in the story.
f _ _ _ _ _ 's

2. Write the four list words that show **belonging to**.

3. Write the four list words that have long **o** spelled **o** _ **e**.

4. Write the two list words with three syllables.

5. Write the list words that fit the blanks.

a) Tie the ropes <u>t</u> _ _ _ <u>t</u> _ _ <u>r</u> .

b) Sarah's dog ran <u>a</u> _ _ _ _ <u>d</u> the tree.

c) Have <u>a</u> _ _ <u>t</u> _ _ <u>r</u> piece of fruit.

d) It's my turn to wash dishes <u>a</u> _ _ _ <u>n</u> !

Word Power

Don't forget to use an **apostrophe**!

1. Change each sentence so that one word means **belonging to**. Write the sentences.

   a) The bone belongs to the dog.
   It is the <u>dog's</u> bone.

   b) The skis belong to my sister.
   They are my _____ skis.

   c) The book belongs to my mother.
   It is my _____ book.

   d) The dish belongs to the kitten.
   It is the _____ dish.

2. Write the words that fit the blanks. They all have the long **o** sound spelled **o _ e**.

   a) I ran all the way <u>h _ m _</u> .

   b) The dog was tied with a <u>r _ p _</u> .

   c) Water your lawn with a <u>h _ s _</u> .

   d) Would you like an ice cream <u>c _ n _</u> ?

   e) We laughed at the funny <u>j _ k _</u> .

3. Unscramble the list word on each bone. Write the words.

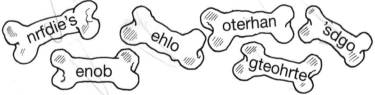

nrfdie's

enob

ehlo

oterhan

gteohrte

sdgo

4. a) Write sentences using three of the words on the bones above.

   b) Read your sentences to a friend. Did you remember to put a capital on the first word?

SUPER
★ ★ ★ ★ ★

imagine
slice
gnome
shadow
garage
grandfather's

★ ★ ★ ★ ★
WORDS

Challenges with Words

1. Unscramble the Super Words on each slice of pie.
Write the words.

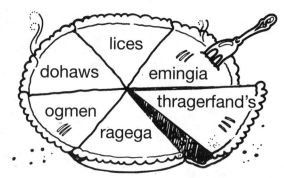

lices
dohaws
emingia
thragerfand's
ogmen
ragega

2. Complete the sentences with Super Words.
Write the words.

a) When I grow up, I want to be a mechanic
and have a _____ of my own.

b) May I have another _____ of pizza,
please?

c) My _____ beard is as white as snow.

3. Use the clues to write words that have the
long **o** sound as in **open** spelled **o _ e.**

a) something you talk on _ _ _ _ _ _ _ o _ e

b) an imaginary creature _ _ o _ e

c) something that fire makes _ _ o _ e

d) a round map of the world _ _ o _ e

4. Use the clues to write words that end in **ow**.

a) a dark shape on the floor

_ _ _ _ ow

b) lets sunlight into the house

_ _ _ _ ow

c) nothing in the middle; empty

_ _ _ _ ow

d) a cushion to use in bed

_ _ _ _ ow

5. Choose four people in your class. Write sentences about something that belongs to each of them. Use their names in your sentences.

Example   Tania's book is on the floor.

6. Use the clues to find one of your Super Words. Write each letter, then unscramble them.

My third letter is in **tastier** but not in **tastiest**.
My second letter is in **images** but not **shimmering**.
My first letter is in **goats** but not in **toast**.
My fifth letter is in **together** but not in **other**.
My sixth letter is in **mechanic** but not in **matching**.
My fourth letter is in **shadow** but not in **showered**.
What am I?   _ _ _ _ _ _
                1 2 3 4 5 6

7. a) Write an imaginary story. Use as many of the Super Words as you can. Think of a scary or funny sentence to start your story.

b) Read your story to a friend.

23

Base Words and Endings
-ing
giv**ing**

| garden |
| giving |
| caring |
| farmer |
| hungry |
| cookies |
| having |
| winter |
| doctor |
| woman |
| coming |
| angry |

See the Words

1. Look at each word in the list.

2. Look at the words. Notice the base word in each one.

   giving—give   having—have

   caring—care   coming—come

   What happens to the base word when we add -**ing** to words ending in **e**?

Say the Words

Say the words. Listen for each sound.

caring	having	giving	coming
angry	hungry	woman	winter
garden	farmer	cookies	doctor

✓ Precheck

Check your work. Underline the parts of the words you need to study.

★ Powerbooster ★

When we add -**ing** to base words that end in **e**, we drop the **e** before adding -**ing**.

Write the Words

1. a) Read the story.

Long ago a woman named Nina lived in the country. She was a farmer. Then she moved to the city and grew vegetables in her tiny backyard. She loved caring for growing things. In the fall, she would pick vegetables and freeze them for the winter. Nina was very healthy and never went to the doctor.

Nina's neighbours liked coming to visit. She was always giving them baskets of vegetables or making homemade cookies for the hungry kids.

Everyone loved Nina's garden. It was like having a piece of the country in city.

b) Look for the list words in the story.
Write them in your notebook.

c) Write the list word that is not in the story.
a _ _ _ y

2. a) Write the four list words that end in **-ing**.
b) Write the base word for each one.

3. Write the two list words that end with the long **e** sound as in **me**. Circle the letter that spells the long **e**.

4. Write the words that fit the boxes.

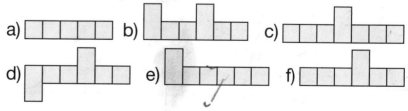

a) b) c)

d) e) f)

Word Power

1. Add -**ing** to the base words on each garden vegetable. Write the words.

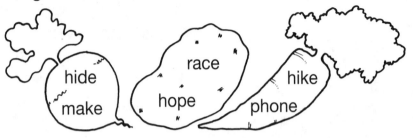

2. Complete the sentences with words that end in a **vowel** + **r**. Write the words.

a) A <u>d a n c e r</u> is someone who dances.

b) An _ _ _ <u>o r</u> is someone who acts.

c) A _ _ _ <u>e r</u> is someone who dives.

d) A _ _ _ _ _ <u>e r</u> is someone who swims.

e) A _ _ _ _ _ <u>e r</u> is someone who teaches.

I need a list word to fit 3a) that means **something to eat**.

3. Complete each set with a list word.

a) cakes   pies   muffins   _____

b) field   meadow   yard   _____

c) mother   lady   aunt   _____

d) spring   fall   summer   _____

e) upset   hurt   annoyed   _____

4. Write about the work a farmer does. Write about a doctor's work. You could begin like this.

A farmer is very important _____ because _____.

SUPER
★ ★ ★ ★ ★
joking
sharing
buying
vegetables
potatoes
actor
★ ★ ★ ★ ★
WORDS

Challenges with Words

1. Write the Super Words that fit these clues.

   a) This word is plural and has ten letters.
   b) This word ends with a **vowel** + **r**.
   c) This word forms the plural by adding **-es**.
   d) This word has the long **o** sound and ends in -**ing**.
   e) This word begins with two consonants.

2. Unscramble the vegetable words. Write the words.

   rocatsr
   topaetos
   dareshis

   runtisp
   osinon
   nesab

3. a) Add -**ing** to these words. Write the words.

   close   bite   shine   wipe

   use   hope   blame   write

   b) Choose three of your new words. Write a sentence with each one.

4. Write a Super Word to complete each set.

   a) singer   dancer   _____
   b) giving   taking   _____
   c) selling   trading   _____
   d) grains   fruits   _____
   e) turnips   beets   _____
   f) telling   laughing   _____

5. Use the letters of the word **vegetables** to write as many small words as you can.

6. Fill in the blanks with words that rhyme with **buying**. Finish the verse with your own ideas. Write it in your notebook.

flying
crying
sighing
trying
tying
spying

I'm going out and <u>buying</u> ,
An airplane for _____ ,
Some shoelaces for _____ ,
A _____ ,
And a _____ .

7. a) Write two headings in your notebook like this.

Vegetables I like	Vegetables I don't like

b) List the names of all the vegetables you like and don't like under each of the headings. Here are some to choose from.

lettuce   broccoli   carrots   beans

corn   brussels sprouts   celery   cabbage

8. Write the words that fit each set.

a) sang   shouted   talked _____

b) bird's   elephant's   mouse's _____

c) ice cream cone   popsicle   lollipop _____

Kids
WORDS

puppy's
licking
spoke

112

24 Looking Back

STUDY STEPS

look

say

cover

write

check

Here is a list of words from Units 19–23 that may be hard for you.

light	thought	coming	another
stopped	again	decided	machine
friend's	woman	around	does

1. Use the Study Steps for each word. Add some of your own review words to the list.

2. Complete the puzzle with words that have the long **i** sound spelled **igh**. Write the words in your notebook.

		i	g	h	
		i	g	h	
		i	g	h	
		i	g	h	
		i	g	h	
		i	g	h	

   a) after the sun sets
   b) like a strong light
   c) the opposite of low
   d) to hit each other
   e) the opposite of wrong
   f) to make a sad sound

3. Write the words from the list below that have the short **o** sound as in **hot**.

   brought   thought   bought   doughnut

   ought   though   fought   found

4. a) Add -**ing** to these base words.

ing

sit write ride swim live begin shop

   b) Write six more words with -**ing** endings from classroom books or your own writing.

113

Remember that an apostrophe is used to show **belonging to**.

5. Add **'s** to each picture word. Write each sentence.

a) the 🐶 nose was cold.

b) The 👒 corn is growing in the fields.

c) Have you seen the 🪁 string?

d) I wish the 👶 first tooth would come!

6. Complete each sentence with the correct word. Write the words.

a) We _____ our lunches to school.

bought	fought
brought	sought

b) I want to _____ my new shirt.

where	wear
were	ware

c) Would you like _____ cookie?

again	around
about	another

d) Last _____ I went to bed early.

right	night
might	light

7. Look in storybooks in your classroom for words ending in -**ed**. Write ten -**ed** words with the base words beside them.

8. Complete the sentences below with words that end in **-ed**. Write the words.

a) 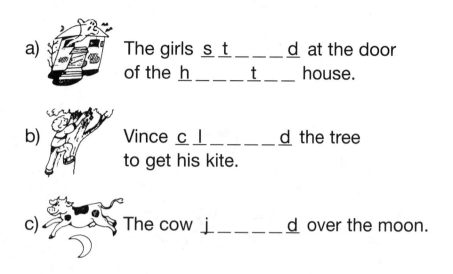 The girls <u>s t</u> _ _ _ <u>d</u> at the door
of the <u>h</u> _ _ _ <u>t</u> _ _ house.

b) Vince <u>c l</u> _ _ _ _ <u>d</u> the tree
to get his kite.

c) The cow <u>j</u> _ _ _ _ <u>d</u> over the moon.

Get a partner
to dictate your
review list to you.

9. Now make your own review list. Use Super
Words, words from your Personal Word List, or
any problem words from Units 19–23. Study
your words using the five Study Steps.

Spring

buds · kites · birds · windy · sunshine · rain · ditch · bikes · tulips · strawberries · fishing · frogs · rubber boots · mud

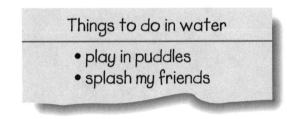

1. Brainstorm with your classmates to find other words that remind you of spring. Make a list or poster of spring words.

Things to do on a rainy spring day	Things to do on a sunny spring day

2. Write these headings in your notebook. Write things you like to do under each heading.

Things to do in water
• play in puddles • splash my friends

3. In spring there is water everywhere. Jot some notes about things you like to do with water.

4. Is it safe to play with the water in ditches and creeks?
Write a safety rule about water in spring.

Grammar Games

Verbs

Present Tense

The **present tense** shows action that is going on **right now** or **every day**.

> She is **swimming** across the lake.
>
> Earth **turns** around the sun.

Tense is a grammar word that means **time**.

1. Write these sentences using the correct form of the present tense.

   a) Watch out! The lamp **fall/is falling**.

   b) The moon **turn/turns** around Earth.

   c) Where are Ahmad and Steven? They **is riding/are riding** home.

   d) The sun **rise/rises** in the East.

2. Write your own sentences with these verbs in the **present tense**.

   jumping   likes   working   plays

   _____ jumping _____.

Dictionary Games

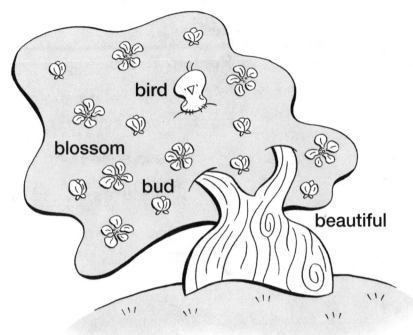

1. Here are some **spring** words that begin with **b**. Put them in alphabetical order.

   1. _____

   2. _____

   3. _____

   4. _____

Remember! Sometimes we have to look at the second letter to put words in alphabetical order.

Proofreading

Read this rough draft of a story. See how many mistakes your proofreader's eye can catch. Write the words correctly.

It's spring agin. All the flowers are comeing up. My friend's garden looks better than mine dose. All I have is mud! That's because our dog is always diging in my mother's flower bed.

25

Short **e**   Vowels with **r**

ea   **ea + r**

h**ea**d   h**ea**rd

---

snow ✓
heard ✓
river ✓
silly ✓
bread ✓
behind ✓
earth ✓
show ✓
head ✓
magic ✓
know ✓
caught ✓

See the Words

Look at each word in the list.

Say the Words

1. Say each word. Listen for each sound.

   earth   heard   bread   head

   behind   show   snow   know

   river   magic   silly   caught

2. Say the words. Listen for the vowel sounds.

   head   bread

   What letters spell the short **e** sound as in **let**?

3. Say the words. Listen for the vowel sounds.

   earth   heard

   What letters spell the short **e** + **r** sound as in **learn**?

☑ Precheck

Check your work. Write the words you misspelled.

★ Powerbooster ★

In some words like **head** we spell the short **e** sound with **ea**.

In some words such as **earth**, we spell the short **e** + **r** sound with **ea** + **r**.

Write the Words

1. a) Read the story.

Last week, I <u>heard</u> that my friend <u>caught</u> fifteen fish in the middle of winter. It sounds <u>silly</u>, I <u>know</u>, but wait... she was ice fishing. Fishing through the ice on a frozen <u>river</u> or lake is lots of fun. You leave the city <u>behind</u> and <u>head</u> for a world of <u>snow</u> and ice. You cut a hole in the ice, then sit and wait for the magic <u>moment</u> when a fish pulls at your line. It's so quiet, it's like you are the only person on <u>earth</u>.

b) Look for the list words in the story. Write them in your notebook.

c) Write the list words that are not in the story.
b _ _ _ d   s _ _ w

2. Write the two list words that have the short **e** sound as in **let** spelled **ea**.

3. Write the two list words that have the short **e** + **r** sound as in **her.**

4. Write the words that have the long **o** spelled **ow.**

5. Write the list words that fit the boxes.

a) I ☐☐☐☐ a fish in the ☐☐☐☐☐ .

b) The boy ☐☐☐☐☐☐ me makes faces. ☐☐☐☐

c) I like to do ☐☐☐☐☐ tricks.

What list word can I make with these letters? g-t-h-a-u-c.

Word Power

1. Unscramble the list words. Write the words.

gthauc   rahed   hdnbei   cagmi

2. Many compound words can be made with the word **snow**. Write compound words for the pictures below.

ear
heard
early
spear
earn
tear
learn

3. Complete the sentences with words from the box that have the short **e** + **r** sound.

a) I _____ the music last night.

b) We left _____ in the morning for school.

c) My sister got a job to _____ some money.

d) My cousin wants to _____ to play the violin.

4. Make words using the word wheel. Write the words.

5. Write sentences using each pair of words below.

bread   spread   heavy   head

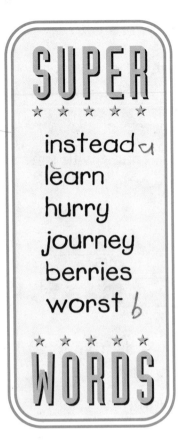

SUPER
★ ★ ★ ★ ★
instead
learn
hurry
journey
berries
worst
★ ★ ★ ★ ★
WORDS

Challenges with Words

1. Complete these sentences with Super Words. Write the words.

a) I would like ice cream _____ of cake, please.
b) This is the _____ hamburger I have ever eaten!
c) Would you like some _____ on your cereal?
d) Do not _____ when you are eating.
e) You can _____ to play hockey.

2. Complete the puzzle with Super Words. Write the words in your notebook.

			r				
			r				
			r				
			r				

a) a long trip
b) go quickly
c) straw_____; blue_____
d) opposite of best

3. How many different kinds of berries can you think of? Write as many as you can in a list.

4. Find words spelled with **rr** to match the meanings. Write the words.

_ _ rr _   a) go fast
_ _ rr _   b) small juicy fruit
_ _ _ _ _ rr _ _   c) small animal with a bushy tail
_ _ rr _   d) ship to carry cars and people
_ _ rr _   e) feel uneasy; care about

5. Write these **worst** sentences in your notebook. Finish them with your own ideas.

a) The worst season is _____ because _____.
b) The worst food is _____ because _____ .
c) The worst thing to touch is _____ because _____

Be careful! Just write the words that match the sound at the top of each box.

6. Make words by joining the letters **ea** with those in the big box. Write the words.

a) short **e** as in **head**

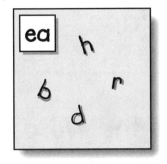

ea h b r d

b) short **e** + **r** as in **learn**

ear n l d ch s h

c) long **e** + **r** as in **ear**

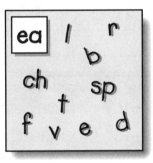

ea l r b ch sp t f v e d

d) long **a** + **r** as in **bear**

ear b p t w

7. a) Write instructions for making the **worst** pie you can imagine. Use as many Super Words as you can.

b) Trade your recipe with a partner. Which recipe is the worst?

8. Write the words that fit the blanks in the story below.

One day our pet bird, Smokey, got lost. We called everyone we knew to help <u>s _ _ _ _ _ h</u> for her. At ten o'clock, my brother <u>b _ _ _ _ t</u> through the door "I have <u>s _ _ _ _ r</u> news " he cried. "Smokey has been found."

Kids WORDS

super
search
burst

26

Sounds of c
k - **c**lown
s - fa**c**e

prince
clown
talk
face
castle
cold
walked
race
police
candy
elephant
dance

See the Words

Look at each word in the list.

Say the Words

1. Say each word. Listen for each sound.

clown   candy   castle   cold
prince   face   race   police
dance   walked   talk   elephant

2. Say the words. Listen for the first consonant sound.

clown   castle   cold

What letter spells the **k** sound in these words?

3. Say the words. Listen for the final consonant sound.

prince   face   police   dance

What letter spells the **s** sound in these words?

✓ Precheck

Check your work. Underline the parts of the words you need to study.

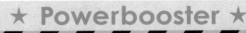

★ Powerbooster ★

In some words the letter **c** spells the consonant sound **k**, and in some words the letter **c** spells the consonant sound **s**.

Write the Words

1. a) Read the story.

Last year, I went to a fair. It was a really <u>cold</u> day, but I had fun. I <u>walked</u> around a storybook <u>castle</u>. There was a <u>clown</u> doing <u>face</u> painting. There was a boy dressed like a <u>prince</u>, reading stories to the kids. A <u>police</u> officer came to <u>talk</u> about bike safety.

In the afternoon there was a three-legged <u>race</u> for the kids. At night there was a <u>dance</u> for the grown-ups. I had such a good time, even though I ate too much <u>candy</u>.

b) Look for the list words in the story. Write them in your notebook.

c) Write the list word that is not in the story.
e _ _ _ _ _ _ t

2. Write the list words that have the **k** sound spelled with **c**.

3. Write the list words that have the **s** sound spelled with **c**.

4. Write the list words that fit the boxes.

a) I like to ⬚⬚⬚⬚ to my friends.

b) We ⬚⬚⬚⬚⬚ to the zoo to see the ⬚⬚⬚⬚⬚ .

Word Power

1. Complete the sentences with the picture words. Write the sentences.

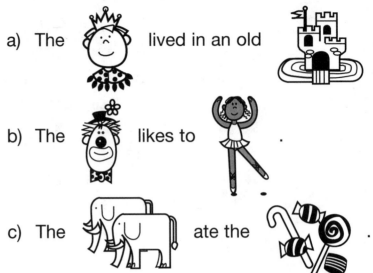

a) The [queen] lived in an old [castle].

b) The [clown] likes to [dance].

c) The [elephants] ate the [candy].

I found **arithmetic** and **space** in my math book.

2. Make two headings in your notebook like the ones below. Find words with the letter **c** in your reading books. Write them under the correct heading.

c with the sound of **k**	c with the sound of **s**

3. Write rhyming words for each of these words.

clown	mice	prince	race	candy
fr _ _ _	tw _ _ _	s _ _ _ _	pl _ _ _	s _ _ _ _

4. Join the two short sentences to make one longer sentence. Write the sentences in your notebook.

a) The castle was cold. The castle was dark.

b) The clown marched in the parade. The police marched in the parade.

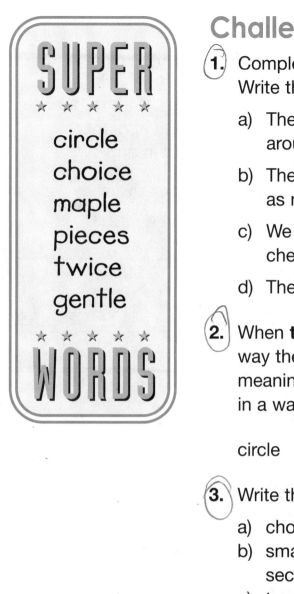

SUPER
★ ★ ★ ★ ★
circle
choice
maple
pieces
twice
gentle
★ ★ ★ ★ ★
WORDS

Challenges with Words

1. Complete these sentences with Super Words. Write the words.

    a) They planted _____ trees in a _____ around the park.

    b) Their _____ of cake are _____ as big as mine.

    c) We had a _____ between crackers or cheese.

    d) The cat was very _____ with her kittens.

2. When **triangle** is written this way the shape is also its meaning. Write these words in a way that shows their shapes.

    circle   square   rectangle

3. Write the Super Words that fit the puzzle.

    a) choosing
    b) small bits or sections
    c) two times
    d) a round shape

				C					
				C					
				C					
				C					

4. Complete the sentences with words that rhyme with **twice**. Write the words.

    a) Cinnamon is a good s _ _ _ _ for cooking.
    b) What is the p _ _ _ _ of that kite?
    c) May I please have a s _ _ _ _ of cheese?
    d) My friend has two pet m _ _ _ .

125

5. Use the clues to write a Super Word.

My third letter is in **name** but not in **mate**.
My fifth letter is in **all** but not in **attack**.
My second letter is in **eat** but not in **train**.
My sixth letter is in **egg** but not in **giant**.
My first letter is in **age** but not in **apple**.
My fourth letter is in **sent** but not in **ends**.
What am I?   _ _ _ _ _ _
                      1 2 3 4 5 6

6. a) Write these headings in your notebook.

c with the sound of **k**	c with the sound of **s**

b) Write each of these words under the correct heading.

came	castle	coat	count
nice	rice	picnic	voice
cent	colour	dance	prince

7. The word **twice** means **two times**. Write three more words that mean something to do with numbers and begin with **tw**.

8. There are many games you play in a circle. Choose your favourite circle game and write a set of rules or instructions for it.

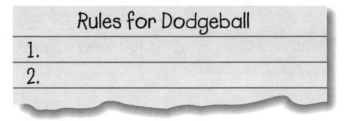

Rules for Dodgeball
1.
2.

27

-ly Endings
happi**ly**

suddenly
animal
finally
tiger
happily
forest
really
gold
sadly
wolf
fox
circus

See the Words

1. Look at each word in the list.

2. Look at each word. Notice what has been added to each base word.
sudden   suddenly   happy   happily

What happens when you add **-ly** to a base word ending in **y**?

Say the Words

1. Say the words. Listen for each sound.

suddenly   finally   happily   really

sadly   animal   tiger   forest

gold   wolf   fox   circus

2. Say the words. Listen for the final consonant sounds.
box   fox   wax

What letter spells the consonant sound **ks** in these words?

✓ Precheck

Check your work. What words do you need to study?

★ Powerbooster ★

When you add **-ly** to a base word ending in **y**, change the **y** to **i**.
In some words the consonant sound **ks** is spelled with the letter **x**.

Write the Words

1. a) Read the story.

Once there was a beautiful <u>tiger</u> who lived in a <u>forest</u>. His black and <u>gold</u> stripes gleamed in the sun. <u>Suddenly</u>, one day a fire broke out in the forest. The tiger was rescued and taken to the zoo. The zoo was not <u>really</u> like the forest, but the tiger lived there <u>happily</u> and made friends with a fox and a <u>wolf</u>.

When the fire <u>finally</u> stopped burning, the tiger was allowed to go home. He was happy to go back to the forest, but <u>sadly</u> had to say goodbye to the <u>animal</u> friends he had made.

b) Look for the list words in the story. Write them in your notebook.

2. a) Write the five list words that end in **-ly**.
   b) Write the base words for each one.

3. Write the picture words.

4. Write the list words that fit the boxes.

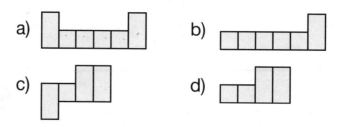

a)   b)

c)   d)

5. Write the four list words that have double consonants.

128

Word Power

1. Solve the puzzle with list words. Write the words.

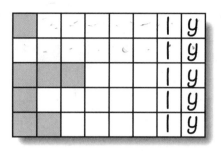

a) at last

b) without warning

c) unhappily

d) with pleasure

e) for sure; definitely

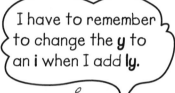

I have to remember to change the **y** to an **i** when I add **ly**.

2. Complete the sentences by adding **-ly** to the word in brackets. Write the words.

a) (Lucky) we did not hurt ourselves when the branch broke.

b) The children danced (merry) in the streets.

c) She yawned (sleepy) at the breakfast table.

3. Write the picture words. They all spell the sound **ks** with the letter **x**.

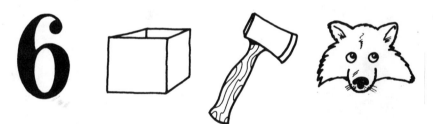

4. Write sentences using each pair of words below. Proofread your sentences with a partner.

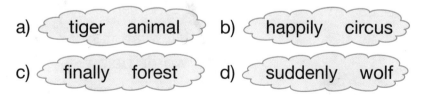

a) tiger animal   b) happily circus

c) finally forest   d) suddenly wolf

SUPER

★ ★ ★ ★ ★

quickly
probably
exciting
accident
exercise
carefully

★ ★ ★ ★ ★

WORDS

Challenges with Words

1. Complete the sentences with Super Words.
Write the words.

a) Be sure to drive ☐☐☐☐☐☐☐ so you

do not have an ☐☐☐☐☐☐☐ .

b) Walking ☐☐☐☐☐☐ is good

☐☐☐☐☐☐☐☐ .

c) This is ☐☐☐☐☐☐ the most

☐☐☐☐☐☐☐ day of my life!

2. Match the **-ly** words in column A with their
opposites in column B. Write each pair of words
in your notebook.

A	B
happily	timidly
carefully	carelessly
slowly	wrongly
boldly	sadly
rightly	quickly

3. Write as many words as you can using the
letters of **carefully.**

4. Write sentences using **exercise** and each of the
words below.

dog   strong   arithmetic

Example My dog needs a lot of exercise.

5. Match the words in the box with their meanings. All of the words spell the sound **ks** with the letter **x**.

a) to look for something new

b) to blow up

c) poisonous

d) a tool for chopping wood

e) to give a reason; to make clear

> axe
> toxic
> explode
> explore
> explain

Ouch! **Accident** reminds me of my hurt knee!

6. Some words make us think of other things. Make a word pole with things the word **accident** reminds you of. The word pole is started for you.

```
    o
    u
a c c i d e n t
    h
```

7. Nathan's bag disappeared when he fell off his bike. Pretend you are a detective. Write about the search for the lost bag. Jot down the steps you take to look for it.

8. Write the words that fit the shapes.

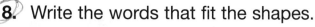

I can ⬚⬚⬚⬚⬚ ⬚⬚⬚⬚⬚ that picture of a ⬚⬚⬚⬚⬚⬚ in my book with tracing paper.

28

Homophones
new   **knew**

---

new
flower
flying
flour
their
to
blew
there
too
blue
knew
crying

See the Words

1. Look at each word in the list.

2. Look at the pairs of words. Say them.

blew blue   new knew   to too   their there

Both words sound the same, but they have different meanings and different spellings. Words like these are called **homophones**.

The sky is **blue.** The wind **blew** all day.

Say the Words

Say each word. Listen for each sound.

crying   flying   there   their

to   too   blew   blue

new   knew   flower   flour

✔ Precheck

Check your work. Write the words you misspelled.

★ Powerbooster ★

Homophones are words that sound alike but have different meanings and spellings. **blew blue**

Write the Words

1. a) Read the conversation.

Bob: Here's a <u>new</u> recipe for chocolate
cake. I'm going <u>to</u> try it out.

Rob: Oh, no! The last time you baked,
<u>flour</u> went <u>flying</u> all over and <u>there</u>
was a huge mess!

Bob: The fan <u>blew</u> the flour. It was <u>too</u>
hot in here so we turned it on,
remember?

Rob: You grabbed that <u>blue</u> cloth and
helped me clean up.

Bob: Mom and Dad never <u>knew</u> <u>their</u>
kitchen had been such a disaster
zone!

b) Look for the list words in the story.
Write them in your notebook.

c) Write the list words that are not in the story.
f _ _ _ _ r   c _ _ _ _ g

2. Complete the sentences with list words. Write
the words.

a) Can I go ⬜ the circus ⬜ ?

b) The wind _ _ _ <u>w</u> my _ _ <u>u</u> _ hat off.

c) We ⬜ the ⬜ teacher.

d) <u>T</u> _ _ _ <u>e</u> goes <u>t</u> _ _ <u>i</u> _ dog.

3. Write the two list words that end in **-ing.**

133

Word Power

1. Look at the picture. Write the word from the box that matches each picture.

their		
there		

a) 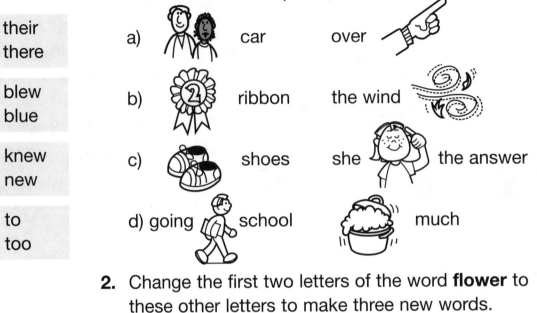 car   over

blew
blue

b) ribbon   the wind

knew
new

c) shoes   she ___ the answer

to
too

d) going ___ school   ___ much

2. Change the first two letters of the word **flower** to these other letters to make three new words.

| fl | ower | | sh | | t | | p |

3. Look at the words in the soup pot. Write the homophones in pairs.

there too bare to
know bear maid
wood made would
here right their
no hear write

4. Write sentences using these pairs of homophones.

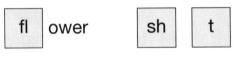

know / no   their / there

SUPER WORDS

dictionary
knot
pair
computer
sentence
alphabet

Challenges with Words

1. Fill in the blanks with Super Words.
Write the words.

a) There are twenty-six letters in the _____ .

b) A _____ is a book with thousands of words and their meanings.

c) A robot is a machine controlled by a _____ .

2. Your computer is having trouble! The words it prints are all scrambled. Unscramble each Super Word.

arpi   mutrepoc   bapehalt

tonk   tencense   rictyadion

3. The Super Words **knot** and **pair** both have **homophones**. Complete the sentences with the correct homophones. Write the sentences.

a) Do (not, knot) untie the (not, knot).

b) I have a new (pair, pear) of shoes.

c) Would you like a juicy (pair, pear)?

4. Write a homophone for each of these words.

a) rode   aunt   son

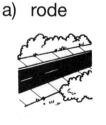      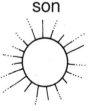

b) flour   for   tale

   4

5. Fill in each blank with a Super Word that goes with the other words in the set. Write the complete sets in your notebook.

a) group   set   _____
b) story   words   _____
c) tangle   loop   _____
d) letters   spelling   _____

6. Using only the letters in the word **computer**, write a word to match each clue.

a) the opposite of **go away**   _ _ _ _ _
b) something you use for **tying**   _ _ _ _ _
c) the opposite of **less**   _ _ _ _ _
d) someone who writes **verses**   _ _ _ _ _

7. Sentences are supposed to make sense, but these sentences got mixed up in the computer. Rewrite the sentences below putting the Super Words in the correct place.

a) I put on a new **alphabet** of shoes and tied them tight with a **sentence**.
b) The **dictionary** printed the first **knot** of the story all wrong.
c) The words in your **pair** are listed in the order of the **computer**.

8. Make a word search with your Super Words and words of your own. Trade your word search with a partner.

Example

s	t	p	a	t	e	u	z	w	v
f	q	a	t	k	n	o	t	x	d
g	z	i	a	p	l	r	t	a	l
l	k	r	n	r	b	c	y	m	o

29

Syllables

di no saurs

barn
beautiful
ugly
open
dinosaurs
room
favourite
hard
reptiles
hospital
body
goodbye

See the Words

Look at each word in the list.

Say the Words

1. Say each word. Listen for each sound.

   hard   barn   ugly   fairy

   lady   hospital   beautiful   favourite

   dinosaurs   room   open   goodbye

2. Say the words. Listen for the number of syllables.

   hospital   beautiful   favourite   dinosaurs

   How many syllables are in each word?

✓ Precheck

Check your work. Underline the parts of the words you need to study.

★ Powerbooster ★

Long words are easier to spell if you divide them into **syllables**.

Write the Words

1. a) Read the dinosaur facts below.

   • <u>Dinosaurs</u> were <u>reptiles</u>. Their name means 'terrible <u>lizards</u>'.
   • Dinosaurs had <u>hard</u> bony skin and strong legs for walking and fighting.
   • The <u>body</u> of a dinosaur could be as small as a van, or as big as a <u>barn</u>.
   • Some dinosaurs could <u>open</u> their mouths extra wide to make <u>room</u> for huge chunks of food.
   • Brontosaurus is a <u>favourite</u> dinosaur of many people. It was not <u>beautiful</u>, but it was not as <u>ugly</u> as stegosaurus, which had sharp spikes on its back.
   • Earth said <u>goodbye</u> to dinosaurs sixty-five million years ago. No one is quite sure why.

   b) Look for the list words in the story. Write them in your notebook.

   c) Write the list word that is not in the story.
   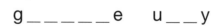
   _ _ s _ _ t _ _

2. Write the five list words that have two syllables.

   o _ _ n   r e p t i l e s   b _ _ y

   g _ _ _ _ _ e   u _ _ y

3. Write the four list words that have three syllables.

   h _ _ p _ _ _ _   b _ _ _ t _ _ _ l

   _ _ n _ s _ _ _ _   f _ _ _ _ r _ _ _

4. Write the two list words that have the sound **ar** as in **star**.

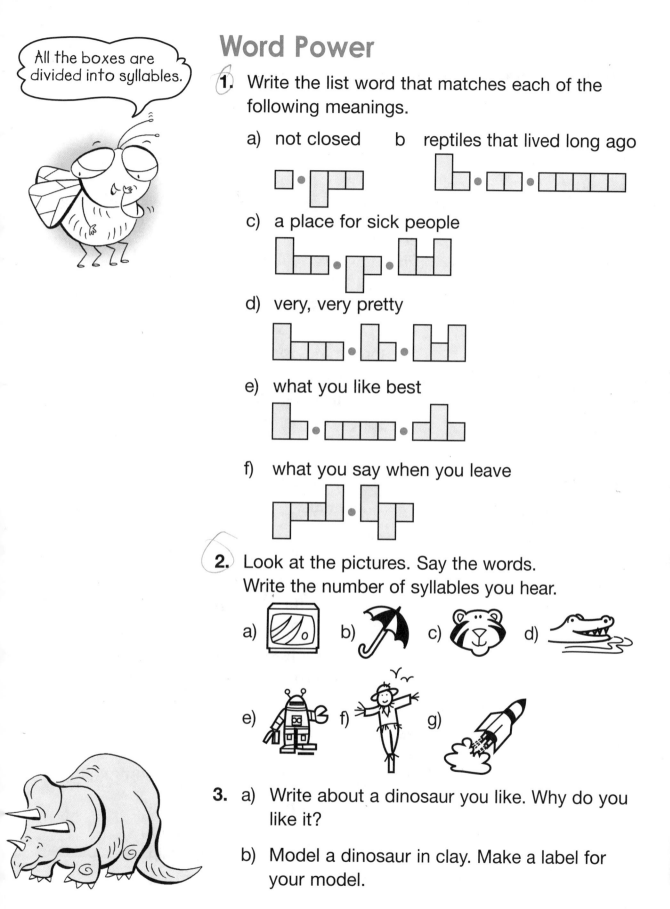

All the boxes are divided into syllables.

Word Power

1. Write the list word that matches each of the following meanings.

a) not closed

b reptiles that lived long ago

c) a place for sick people

d) very, very pretty

e) what you like best

f) what you say when you leave

2. Look at the pictures. Say the words. Write the number of syllables you hear.

a) b) c) d)

e) f) g)

3. a) Write about a dinosaur you like. Why do you like it?

b) Model a dinosaur in clay. Make a label for your model.

Challenges with Words

SUPER
★ ★ ★ ★ ★
liquid
metal
scientist
instrument
inventions
automatic
★ ★ ★ ★ ★
WORDS

1. Use the clues to write the Super Words.

    a) a word with four syllables
    b) three words with three syllables
    c) two words with two syllables

2. Write the Super Word that goes with each meaning.

    a) works by itself
    b) a thing for making music; a tool
    c) new things
    d) steel, gold, copper, etc.
    e) a person who studies science
    f) something you can pour

3. a) Fill in the blanks in this paragraph with Super Words and your own ideas. Write the paragraph.

    Doctor Zeena is an inventor who has many marvellous _____ . She invented an _____ that can measure _____ . Her invention doesn't need anyone to run it. It's _____ . I think Dr. Zeena will be very _____ for many years.

    b) Underline all the words in the paragraph that have more than one syllable. Use a red crayon for two syllables, a blue crayon for three syllables, and a green crayon for four syllables.

4. Write a word ending in **-ist** for each meaning.

    a) a person who studies science
    b) a doctor who looks after teeth
    c) a person who plays the violin
    d) a person who plays the guitar

5. Look at the word and picture clues. Write the musical instrument that fits each line.

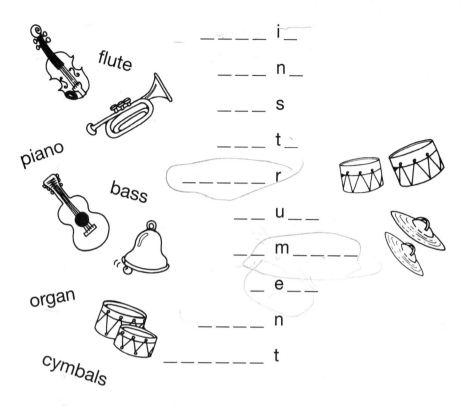

flute

piano

bass

organ

cymbals

_ _ _ _ _ i _

_ _ _ n _

_ _ _ s

_ _ _ t _

_ _ _ _ _ _ r

_ _ u _ _ _

_ _ m _ _ _ _

_ e _ _

_ _ _ _ n

_ _ _ _ _ _ _ t

Kids WORDS

ripped
meat-eater
footprints

6. Imagine you are on a space flight. Danger! The rocket fuel is leaking. Write a story about what is going to happen. Use as many Super Words as you can.

7. Unscramble the words to complete the sentences.

On a dinosaur dig, we found fossil ttfinoospr of a huge dinosaur. Nearby we found its jawbone. It was a eamt - eerta. Its long sharp teeth ppdrie the flesh of its prey.

30

STUDY STEPS

look

say

cover

write

check

Looking Back

Here is a list of words from Units 25–29 that may be hard for you.

heard	castle	suddenly	their
know	beautiful	happily	blew
caught	dinosaurs	flour	finally

1. Follow the Study Steps for each word. Your teacher will dictate the words.

2. The balloons have words with the sound **k** as in **cat** or **s** as in **ice** spelled with **c**. Make two columns in your notebook and write the words under the correct heading.

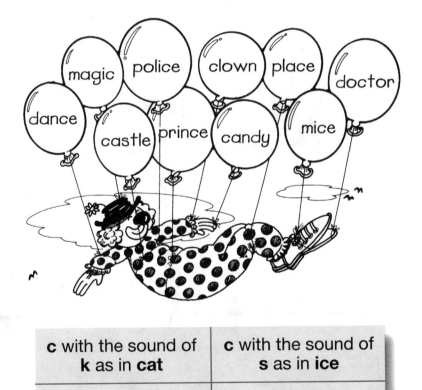

c with the sound of **k** as in **cat**	**c** with the sound of **s** as in **ice**
clown	police

3. **a)** Write the words that have the short **e** sound as in **let**.

heard   head   bread   heat

b) Write the words with the long **e** sound as in **me**.

leaves   meal   seat   earth   head

c) Write the words with the short **e** + **r** sound as in **earn**.

earth   lean   heard   learn   clean

4. Complete each sentence with the correct homophone. Write the sentences.

a) (There, Their) is a party at (there, their) house today.
b) Is that my hat over (there, their)?
c) The girl in the (blew, blue) shirt (blew, blue) bubbles.
d) I (knew, new) that I would get a (knew, new) bike.
e) You are going (to, too) be sick if you eat (too, to) much candy.
f) I would like to come (too, to).

5. Add **-ly** to the following words.
sad   happy   kind   merry

6. Complete the puzzle with words that have the long **o** sound spelled **ow**. Write the words in your notebook.

c	r		
	l		
g	r		
	s		
s	n		
g	l		

a) a large black bird
b) not high
c) to get bigger
d) to plant seeds
e) what rain turns to in winter
f) to shine in the dark

7. a) Write these headings in your notebook.

People	Animals	Buildings	Food

What strategies do you use to learn 'tricky' words?

b) Write each of these words under the correct heading.

castle	prince	tiger	candy	bread
fox	police	hospital	school	clown
lady	house	barn	cookies	meat

8. On your review list you can put words you misspelled on the Unit Tests, words from your Personal Word List, or Super Words.
Study your words using the five Study Steps.
Find a partner to dictate your words to you.

Sea Adventures

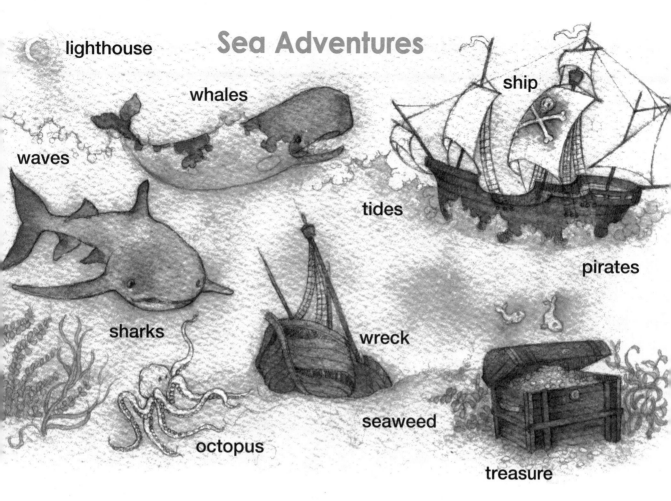

lighthouse
whales
waves
ship
tides
pirates
sharks
wreck
octopus
seaweed
treasure

1. Brainstorm to find other words that remind you of the sea. Make a class list of **sea words** to use in your own writing.

2. You are wearing your diving suit and exploring the sea bottom. Describe what you can see and feel as you swim along. Draw a picture of yourself as a deep sea diver.

3. Imagine you are one of these sea creatures.

   a great white shark   a porpoise
   an octopus   a whale

   a) Write about an adventure under the sea.

   b) Make a poster or mural to illustrate your writing.

Grammar Games

Adverbs

Adverbs are words that describe verbs.
Many adverbs end in **ly**.

She went **quickly**.

He sang **loudly**.

1. Match the adverbs in column A with the actions in column B.

A	B
run	loudly
talk	quickly
shout	quietly
ride	swiftly
walk	slowly

Verbs in the Past

Most verbs add **-ed** to show that an action took place in the past. Some verbs have special past forms.

Example   go ... went
          The ship **went** as far as South America.

2. a) Use the past tense verbs in the box to complete this story.

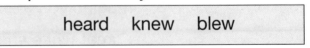

heard   knew   blew

The wind _ _ _ _ harder. The sailors
_ _ _ _ _ _ the captain shout, "Courage!"
The captain _ _ _ _ they could bring the
ship through the storm.

Dictionary Games

smokestack

ship

sea

sand

Don't forget! When you are putting words in alphabetical order and they start with the same first letter, look at the second letter.

1. Write the words in the picture in alphabetical order.

1. _____

2. _____

3. _____

4. _____

2. Choose three people to go on a boat ride with you. Write their names on a passenger list. Remember, the names must be in alphabetical order.

Example

Passenger List

1. Alissa

2. Jermaine

3. Sandik

31

Math Words
eight

eight
second
fifteen
million
math
guess
buy
metre
through
dollars
hundred
thousand
grade

✓ Precheck

Check your work. Write the words you misspelled.

See the Words

1. Look at each word in the list.

2. Look at the words.

   fifteen   sixteen   seventeen

   What is the ending for the number words between twelve and twenty?

Say the Words

1. Say each word. Listen for each sound.

   eight   grade   second   guess

   fifteen   metre   million   math   buy

   through   dollars   hundred   thousand

2. Say the words. Listen for the first vowel sound.

   eight   eighty   neighbour

   What letters spell the long **a** sound as in **age**?

★ Powerbooster ★

The numbers 13, 14, 15, 16, 17, 18, 19 are written with the ending **teen**.

In some words the letters **eigh** spell the long **a** as in **age**.

Write the Words

1. a) Read this dialogue between Mike and Rajit at the corner store.

  Mike: I'd like to <u>buy</u> that soccer ball, but it costs <u>fifteen</u> <u>dollars</u>. I only have <u>eight</u>!

  Rajit: Just a <u>second</u>! That sign says, "<u>Guess</u> the number of beans in the <u>metre</u> high jar and win a soccer ball."

  Mike: I can't get <u>through</u> <u>grade</u> three <u>math</u>, so how can I count a <u>million</u> jelly beans?

  Rajit: You don't have to count them. Just guess. I think there must be six <u>hundred</u> jelly beans.

  Mike: Well, I guess one <u>thousand</u>.

  b) Look for each list word in the story. Write them in your notebook.

2. Write the list words that are number words.

3. Write the list words that fit the boxes.

a)

b)

c)

d)

4. Write the list words that rhyme with each of these words.

   mess   sky   blue   callers

Word Power

1. Write the words for each of these number terms.

   a) 8   15   100   1000
   b) 18   16 $8.00   2nd

2. Unscramble the list words. Write the words.

   a) temre   b) sathduon   c) illniom
   d) ghiet   e) rhugtho

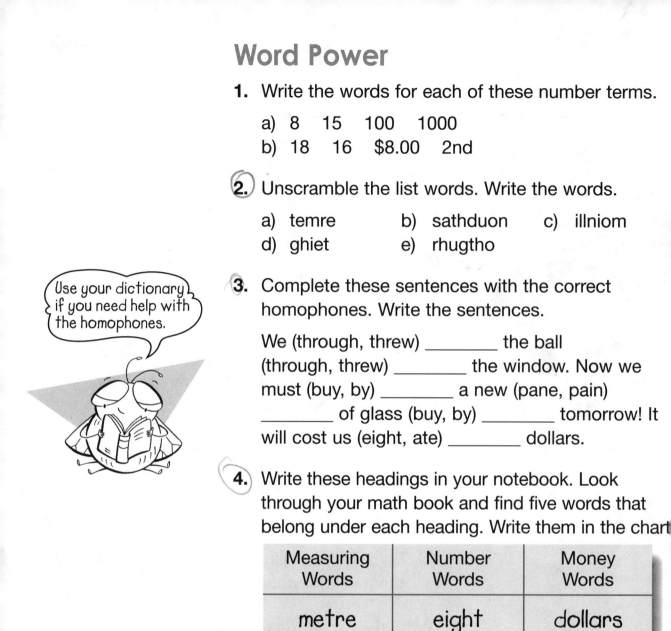

Use your dictionary if you need help with the homophones.

3. Complete these sentences with the correct homophones. Write the sentences.

   We (through, threw) _____ the ball (through, threw) _____ the window. Now we must (buy, by) _____ a new (pane, pain) _____ of glass (buy, by) _____ tomorrow! It will cost us (eight, ate) _____ dollars.

4. Write these headings in your notebook. Look through your math book and find five words that belong under each heading. Write them in the chart.

Measuring Words	Number Words	Money Words
metre	eight	dollars

5. Write a dialogue between you and a friend. Try to use as many math words as you can.

   You: _____
        _____.

   Your _____
   friend: _____.

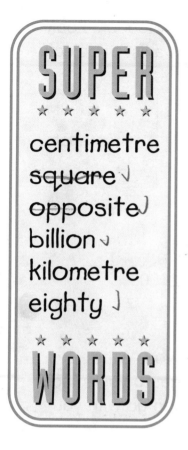

SUPER
★ ★ ★ ★ ★
centimetre
square ✓
opposite ✓
billion ✓
kilometre
eighty ✓
★ ★ ★ ★ ★
WORDS

Challenges with Words

1. Complete these sentences with Super Words. Write the words.

   a) My finger is about one _____ across.

   b) The _____ table cost _____ dollars.

   c) Does right mean the _____ of left?

   d) He runs a _____ every morning.

   e) There are more than a _____ people in China.

2. Unscramble the Super Words. Write the words.

   nollibi ✓   sopitoep ✓   quersa ✓

   mectitrene   giteyh   treklimeo

3. Write sentences with the Super Words. See if you can fit them all in one or two sentences.

4. Write the Super Words in order from shortest to longest.

Use a dictionary to find the meaning of words you do not know.

5. Match the words in list A with the words that mean the **opposite** in list B. Write the pairs in your notebook.

A	B
calm ✓	same
arrive ✓	expensive ✓
cheap ✓	ancient ✓
modern ✓	stormy ✓
opposite	leave ✓

6. Write these headings in your notebook. Look around your classroom. Make a list of objects that are these shapes.

square   round   rectangle

7. Write these number words.

a) 1000   d) 18

b) 12   e) 2000

c) 14   f) 100

8. a) Your friend wants to visit you. Write directions telling how to get to your place from school. Draw a map to go with your directions.

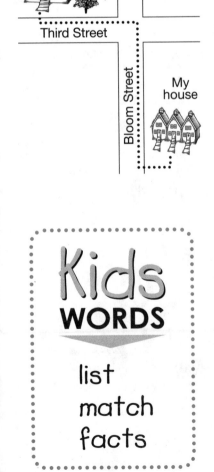

Example   Walk out of the school.
Turn left. Walk to Bloom Street.
Turn right...

b) Go over the map with a partner. Is it easy to understand?

9. Write the words that fit the boxes to complete these sentences.

a) She knows her number ⬜⬜⬜ very well.

b) She can ⬜⬜⬜ the questions with the answers and write them in a ⬜⬜⬜.

Kids WORDS

list
match
facts

150

32

Plurals
dishes   babies

brush
babies
eyes
grey
great
noise
dishes
okay
kittens
days
girls
watch
bears

✓ Precheck

Check your work. What words do you need to study?

See the Words

1. Look at each word in the list.

2. Look at each base word and its plural.

   baby   babies   lady   ladies

   What happens to the base word when forming the plural of these words?

3. Look at each base word and its plural.

   dish   dishes   catch   catches

   What letters are added to form the plural of these words?

Say the Words

Say the words. Listen to each sound.

grey   great   bears   brush

babies   eyes   days   noise   dishes

okay   kittens   girls   watch

★ Powerbooster ★

We write the plural of most words by adding **-s**.

But – if a word ends in a **consonant** + **y**, we change **y** to **i** and add **-es**.

– if a word ends in **sh** or **ch** we add **-es**.

Write the Words

1. **a)** Read the story.

Three grey kittens with green eyes
lived with Nikos and Maria. They liked to
brush the kittens' fur and take them
outside on nice days to play. One day
they heard a great noise in the kitchen.
They rushed in and found dishes all over
the floor.

"Watch out!" cried Nikos. "It looks like
the three bears have been in here!"

"It's okay," said his sister. "They're just
babies. They didn't mean to make a
mess."

b) Look for the list words in the story.
Write them in your notebook.

c) Write the list word that is not in the story.

g _ _ _ s

2. Write the seven list words that are plural.

3. Write the five list words that have the
long **a** sound as in **cake**.
Circle the letters in each word that spell long **a**.

4. Write the list words that fit the boxes.

a) 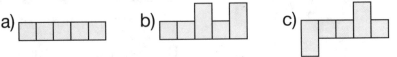 b) c)

5. Write the list words that start with consonant
blends.

Word Power

1. Write the plural for each picture word.

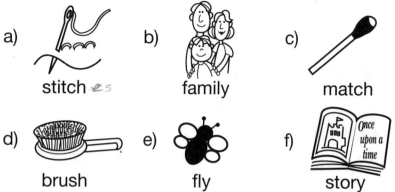

a) stitch *es*   b) family   c) match

d) brush   e) fly   f) story

Hint! Sometimes you will have to take out or change a word when you make other words plural.

2. Make the underlined words plural. Write the sentences. You may have to change other words to make each new sentence correct.

a) The <u>brush</u> is dirty. The <u>brushes are</u> dirty.
b) The <u>baby</u> made a funny <u>noise</u>.
c) My aunt told a <u>story</u> about a <u>bear</u>.
d) My <u>aunt</u> bought one <u>watch</u>.

3. Make each animal or bird name plural. Write sentences using each new plural you have made.
Example

finch   The finches are flying from tree to tree.

a) ostrich   b) monkey

c) pony   d) rhinoceros

153

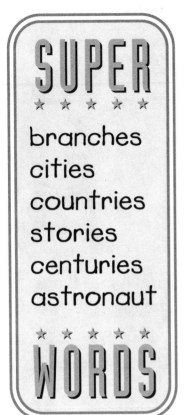

SUPER
★ ★ ★ ★ ★

branches
cities
countries
stories
centuries
astronaut

★ ★ ★ ★ ★

WORDS

Challenges with Words

1. Use the clues to write the Super Words.
    a) words that form the plural by changing **y** to **i** and adding **-es**
    b) a word that forms the plural by adding **-es**
    c) a word that forms the plural by adding **-s**

2. Complete these sentences with Super Words. Write the sentences.

    a) The _____ saw many _____ and _____ as the spaceship circled Earth.

    b) The _____ of the tree swayed in the breeze.

    c) These _____ were written two _____ ago.

Hint! The capital letter is the first letter of each word.

3. Unscramble the names of these Canadian cities. Write the names. Each is the capital city of a province.

    a) geRnia   b) faliHax
    c) roTootn   d) beuQce tyCi
    e) monEnodt   f) Friedcreton
    g) lottenotwCahr   h) ctVriiao
    i) tS. honJ's   j) nniWpige

4. Write these Super Words so they mean **one**.

    branches cities countries stories centuries

5. Change the words in brackets to plurals. Write the words.

a) We saw many _____ (flash) of lightning.

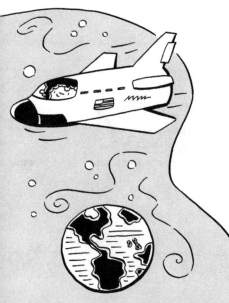

b) The _____ (battery) in my flashlight are getting weak.

c) Those _____ (bully) don't frighten me!

d) Those _____ (bush) have beautiful flowers in spring.

e) I wish I could have three _____ (wish).

6. Write your own fill-in-the-blank sentences with the Super Words. Trade them with a partner.

7. a) Imagine that you are an astronaut in space. Send a report back to your control centre telling what you see. Use as many Super Words as you can.

> Control centre: What do things look like from up there?
>
> Astronaut: Great! I'm looking down at _____.

b) Share reports with a small group. Write a group dialogue about a space voyage.

33

See the Words

Look at each word in the list.

Say the Words

1. Say the words. Listen for each sound.

pool   moon   soon   true   air

hair   chair   television   field

ground   world   wants   clothes

2. Say the words. Listen for the vowel sounds.

moon   soon   pool

What letters spell the long **u** sound as in **rule**?

3. Say the words. Listen for the **vowel** + **r** sound.

air   hair   chair

What letters spell the long **a** + **r** sound as in **bear**?

---

television
pool
hair
moon
field
soon
ground
world
true
air
chair
clothes
wants

✓ Precheck

Check your work. Underline the parts of the words you need to study.

★ Powerbooster ★

In some words the letters **oo** spell the long **u** sound as in **moon**.

Sometimes the long **a** + **r** sound as in **bear**, is spelled with the letters **air** as in **chair**.

156

Write the Words

1. a) Read the sentences.

Last night I saw a <u>television</u> show about creatures who live on a far off <u>moon</u>. In their <u>world</u> the <u>air</u> always smells like popcorn. Each creature has a flying <u>chair</u> that takes it wherever it <u>wants</u> to go. Each house has a <u>pool</u> where the creatures wash their green <u>clothes</u> and purple <u>hair</u>. Outside, in a <u>field</u>, food pops out of the <u>ground</u>, ready to eat. Of course, I don't believe the TV show was <u>true</u>.

b) Look for the list words in the story. Write them in your notebook.

c) Write the list word that is not in the story.
s _ _ n

2. Write the four list words that have the long **u** sound as in **rule**. Circle the letters that spell the long **u** sound.

3. Write the three list words that rhyme with **bear**.

4. Write the list words that fit the blanks.

a) She <u>w _ _ _ _ s</u> new <u>c _ _ _ _ _ _ s</u> for the party.

b) I like to sit in this <u>c _ _ _ _ r</u> when I watch <u>t _ l _ v _ s _ _ _</u>.

c) Astronauts can see the whole <u>w _ _ _ d</u> from space.

d) We planted seeds in the <u>g _ _ _ _ _ d</u> .

e) The football <u>f _ _ _ d</u> was wet and muddy.

Don't forget! **oo** often makes the long **u** sound as in **toot** and **boot**.

Word Power

1. Complete the puzzle with words that have the long **u** sound as in **rule**. Write the words in your notebook.

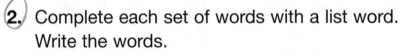

s	p				
	m				
	h				
	t				
b	r				

a) you use this to eat soup
b) it provides light at night
c) the sound an owl makes
d) used for chewing and biting
e) used for sweeping floors

2. Complete each set of words with a list word. Write the words.

a) stars   sun   planets   _____

b) Earth   globe   _____

c) radio   stereo   movies   _____

d) bed   sofa   table   _____

e) nails   skin   eyebrows   _____

3. Add letters to **air** to make new words. Write the words in your notebook.

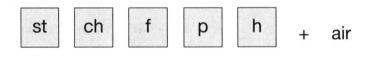

| st | ch | f | p | h | + air |

4. Write sentences using the word pairs below. Then, read them to a partner.

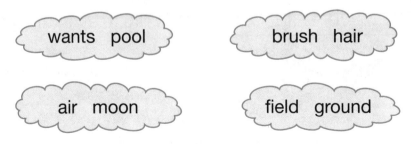

wants   pool

brush   hair

air   moon

field   ground

158

SUPER

★ ★ ★ ★ ★

loose
spooky
scary
fair
buried
tools

★ ★ ★ ★ ★

WORDS

Challenges with Words

1. Replace the vowels in these Super Words.
Write the words.

f _ _ r   t _ _ ls   b _ r _ _ d

l _ _ s _   sp _ _ ky   sc _ ry

2. Complete the sentences with Super Words.
Write the words.

a) We_____ our toys in the sand
and couldn't find them!

b) I need the proper _____ to fix
the _____ wheel on my bike.

c) It was very _____ going through
that _____ haunted house!

You can use your
dictionary to help
you spell the names
of the tools.

3. Tools are what people use to do their work.
Make a list of tools that are needed by the
following people. Add other people and tools to
the chart.

People	Tools
carpenter	
gardener	
painter	

159

Don't forget! Your rhyming words don't have to be spelled the same.

4. Brainstorm with a partner to find words that rhyme with these words. Write as many words as you can.

loose   tools   scary   fair

5. a) Imagine you have found this old map that shows you the location of a buried treasure. Ask yourself
- Who put the treasure there?
- Why was it buried?
- What is it?

b) Write a story about searching for the treasure.

6. Write the words that fit the clues below.

a) I'm a word that means the flat sandy shore of an ocean or a lake. _____

b) I'm a word that is the opposite of midnight.

_____

c) I'm a word that means young dogs. _____

Kids
WORDS

puppies
beaches
noon

-ed Endings Contractions
tri**ed**   **wasn't**

even
wasn't
while
doesn't
party
tried
kite
cried
floor
dollar
cheese
planet
think

✓ Precheck

Check your work. Write the words you misspelled.

See the Words

1. Look at each word in the list.

2. Look at the words. Notice the apostrophe.

   wasn't   doesn't

   Remember that the apostrophe takes the place of a letter in a contraction.

3. Look at the words.
   cry + ed = cried
   try + ed = tried

   What happens to the base word when we add **-ed** to a word ending in a **consonant** + **y**?

Say the Words

Say the words. Listen for each sound.

wasn't   doesn't   tried   cried

while   kite   think   even   cheese

party   floor   dollar   planet

★ Powerbooster ★

When you add **-ed** to words that end in a **consonant** + **y**, change the **y** to **i** before you add the ending, as in the words **cried** and **tried**.

Write the Words

1. a) Read the story.

     My <u>party</u> <u>wasn't</u> going well no matter what I <u>tried</u>! <u>Even</u> handing out <u>cheese</u> sticks didn't help. I wished I was on another <u>planet</u>! I went into the kitchen and sat on the <u>floor</u>. "What am I going to do?" I <u>cried</u>.

     "Sitting there <u>doesn't</u> help," said my little sister Sarah. "Why don't you borrow my new <u>kite</u>?" So we all went outside to fly Sarah's kite and what do you <u>think</u>? It worked! After a <u>while</u> everyone was having fun.

b) Look for the list words in the story. Write them in your notebook.

c) Write the list word that is not in the story.

    d _ _ _ _ _ _

2. Write the two list words that are contractions.

3. Write the two list words that rhyme with **hide**.

4. Write these picture words.

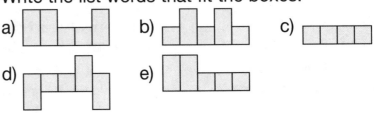

5. Write the list words that fit the boxes.

a)
b)
c)

d)
e)

162

Word Power

1. Add **-ed** to each planet orbiting the sun. Write the words you have made.

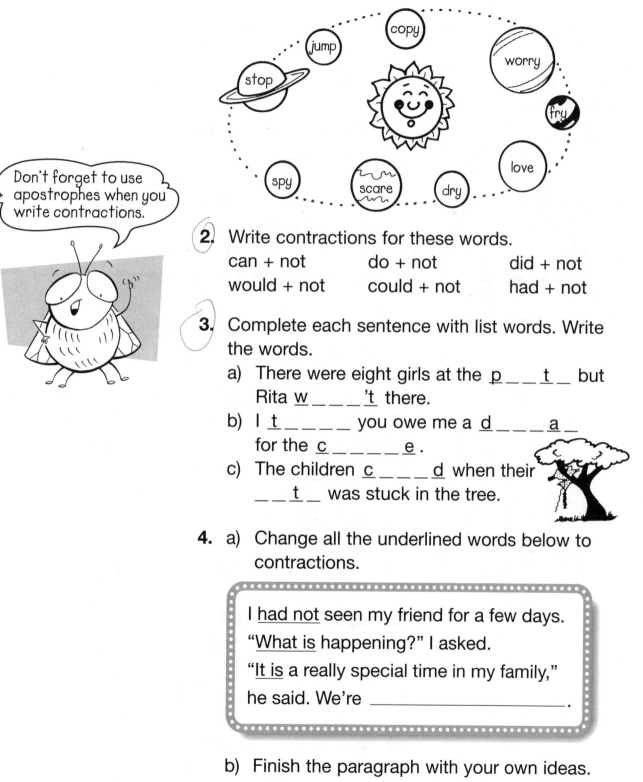

Don't forget to use apostrophes when you write contractions.

2. Write contractions for these words.

can + not	do + not	did + not
would + not	could + not	had + not

3. Complete each sentence with list words. Write the words.
   a) There were eight girls at the p _ _ t _ but Rita w _ _ _ 't there.
   b) I t _ _ _ _ _ you owe me a d _ _ _ _ a _ for the c _ _ _ _ e .
   c) The children c _ _ _ _ d when their _ _ t _ was stuck in the tree.

4. a) Change all the underlined words below to contractions.

   I had not seen my friend for a few days.

   "What is happening?" I asked.

   "It is a really special time in my family," he said. We're _____ .

   b) Finish the paragraph with your own ideas.

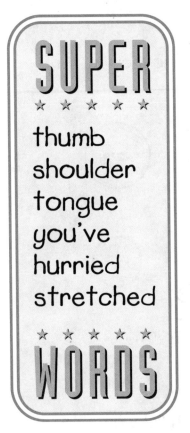

SUPER
★ ★ ★ ★ ★
thumb
shoulder
tongue
you've
hurried
stretched
★ ★ ★ ★ ★
WORDS

Challenges with Words

1. Complete these sentences with Super Words. Write the words.

   a) I hurt my <u>s h</u> _ _ _ _ _ _ and <u>t h</u> _ _ _ when I fell.

   b) <u>Y</u> _ _'_ _ burnt your <u>t</u> _ _ _ _ _ on the hot soup.

   c) When he woke up late, he <u>s t r</u> _ _ _ _ _ _ quickly and <u>h</u> _ _ _ _ _ <u>d</u> to school.

2. To help you remember how to spell **hurried**, look at the Powerbooster rule in this unit. Now, add **-ed** to each of these base words.

   marry   bury   worry   multiply

3. Write an interesting sentence with each word you made in exercise 2.

4. The word **tongue** has many interesting meanings besides the tongue in your mouth. Write in your own words what these phrases mean.

   a) a tongue twister
   b) tongue-tied
   c) hold your tongue

Make a picture of one of these sayings!

5. Complete the sets with Super Words. Write the words.

   a) shrunk   pulled   _____
   b) jaw   cheek   _____
   c) you'll   you'd   _____
   d) toe   finger   _____
   e) hip   elbow   _____
   f) speeded   rushed   _____

6. Write contractions for these pairs of words.

they have	we have	have not
I have	you have	has not

7. Write your own sentence for each contraction you made in exercise 6.

8. a) Invent a creature made from parts of different animals. Give your creature a name.

    b) Draw a picture of it and label all the different parts of its body.

Example   **A Spotted Glopus**

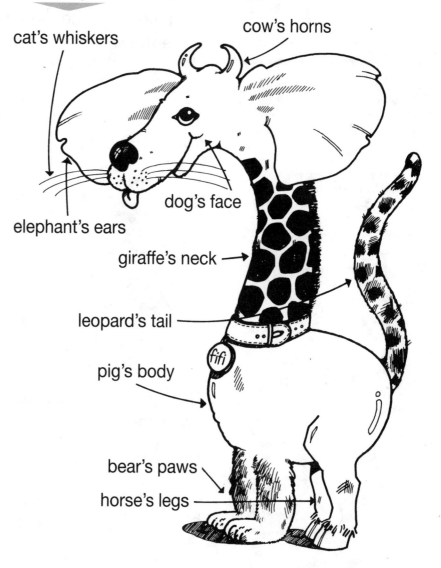

cat's whiskers

cow's horns

dog's face

elephant's ears

giraffe's neck

leopard's tail

pig's body

bear's paws

horse's legs

35

STUDY STEPS

look

say

cover

write

check

Looking Back

Here is a list of words from Units 31–34 that may be hard for you.

eight	through	ground	field
guess	television	clothes	true
tried	doesn't	noise	while

1. Use the Study Steps for each word. Your teacher will dictate the words.

2. Look again at the math words in Unit 31. Write the words that match these symbols.

   $ 8   100   15   2nd   1 000 000

3. The pictures are all plurals. Write the words in your notebook.

   a)

   b)

4. Change these plural forms to mean **only one**. Write the words.

Example	boys	boy
a) churches	babies	ducks
b) planets	dishes	ponies

5. Add **-ed** to each base word. Write the words.

climb	hop	fry
spy	smile	drop

6. Decide which homophone belongs in each sentence. Write the complete sentence in your notebook.

a) There are (ate, eight) pennies in the picture.

b) The ball flew (threw, through) the window.

c) We cut enough (wood, would) for the campfire.

d) The sheepdog had long (hare, hair).

e) Shanti's family went to the store to (buy, by) groceries.

7. Write the words that appear twice in each list.

a)	mood	moon	noon	moon
b)	fair	hair	hare	hair
c)	clothes	cloths	close	clothes
d)	though	through	tough	through

8. Write a sentence for each of your answers in exercise 7.

9. Find **ten** words that mean **only one**. Change each word to the plural form.

Example

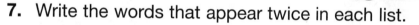

coat   coats

10. Make word pyramids.
Fill in the spaces with words of
your own about **eyes** and **dishes**.

11. Follow the example and write words for these
pictures.

Example

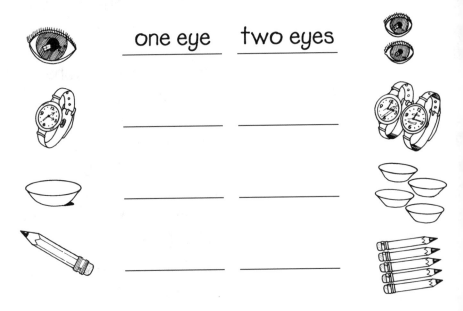

	one eye	two eyes	

I have some special
words of my own
for my review list.

12. Make your own review list. Use words from
your Personal Word List or difficult words from
the Unit Tests. Study your words and have a
partner dictate them to you.

Summer

sunny

August

heat

baseball

camping

mosquitoes

picnic

swimming

holidays

1. Brainstorm to find summer words that you can use in your writing. Make a poster of **summer words**.

2. Write to someone inviting them to spend the summer with you. Tell them about the things that are fun to do in your area.

3. a) Imagine what you are going to do on your summer holiday. Jot notes about where you would like to go or what you would like to do.

   b) Tell a friend about your summer. You can make a tape of your conversation.

Summer Holiday Ideas
• go to the beach
• play in the sand
• ride my bike
• play with my friends

Grammar Games

Joining Sentences

We join two short sentences with **and** if they agree with each other.

Example   We love camping. We go every year.
           We love camping, and we go every year.

We join two short sentences with **but** if they don't agree with each other.

Example   We love picnics. We don't like ants.
           We love picnics, but we don't like ants.

Watch for the comma! When you join two complete sentences, add a comma before **and** or **but**.

1. Write these sentences with **and** or **but**. Don't forget the comma.

   a) We can enjoy playing in parks _____ we should not forget to pick up our litter.
   b) It's important to water the lawn _____ we should not waste water.
   c) We can recycle our paper garbage _____ we can compost our vegetable scraps.

2. Match the sentences below. Join them with **and** or **but**.

Example   They like swimming, and they like riding bikes.

A	B
They like swimming.	They like riding bikes.
They love hiking.	They don't like soccer.
They like snowshoeing.	They don't like camping.
They like baseball.	They like skiing.

Dictionary Games

1. Brainstorm a list of words that have something to do with the environment. Use words that begin with different letters.

air

environment

water

compost

2. Write your words in alphabetical order.

Proofreading

Find the words that are not spelled correctly in this paragraph. Talk to a partner about where the writer made a mistake. Then, write the words correctly.

I gues it's true that our plannet is in trouble, but it doesn't have to be that way. If peeple would just think about the nergy they use and what they throw away, our worlt would soone be a better plase!

Basic Word List

Many of these words are in the list of the 200 most
frequently misspelled words. The words with an * beside
them are in the top 25 most frequently misspelled words.

about
afraid
afternoon
again
ago
air
almost
along
also
always
angry
animal
another
any
anything
around
ask
asked
asleep
ate

babies
bang
barn
baseball
beach
bears
beautiful
because*
been

began
behind
being
best
better
bit
bite
blew
blue
boat
body
bone
books
bought
bread
broke
brought
brush
buy

called
camping
candy
caring
cars
castle
caught*
cave
chair
cheese

circus
class
clean
climbed
clothes
clown
coat
cold
colour
coming
cookies
could
couldn't
cows
cried
crying
cut

dance
days
decided
didn't*
died
dinosaurs
dishes
doctor
does
doesn't
dog's
doing

dollars
done
dragon
duck

earth
eating
egg
eight
elephant
end
even
ever
every
everybody
everyone
everything
eyes

face
fall
far
farmer
fat
favourite
feet
felt
few
field
fifteen

fight	haunted	lake	okay
finally	having	land	once
finished	head	last	only
fire	heard	later	open
first	helped	leaves	our
floor	here	left	
flour	he's	leg	party
flower	high	light	people
fly	hill	looking	pick
flying	himself	looks	picked
forest	hole	loved	planet
fox	holiday	lunch	plant
friend*	hospital		police
friend's	hundred		pond
	hungry	machine	pool
game	hurt	magic	prince
games		many	
garden		math	queen
gave	I'd	may	
gets	I'll	maybe	race
getting	inside	mean	really
girl	its	men	reptiles
girls		met	right
giving	jumped	metre	river
goes	jumps	million	road
gold	just	moon	rock
gone		more	room
goodbye	kept	morning	running
grade	kill	most	runs
great	killed	mother's	
grey	kind	much	
ground	king	must	sadly
guess	kiss	myself	said*
	kite		same
	kittens		sat
hair	kitten's	near	Saturday
happened	knew	new	scared
happily	know	night	second
hard		noise	set
		nose	

sharks	tell	wanted
sharp	ten	wants
ship	than	wasn't
should	that's*	watch
show	their*	wear
sick	there*	week
side	they*	well
silly	they're	were*
sing	think	where*
sitting	those	while
skunk	thought	wild
sky	thousand	wind
small	through	window
smell	tiger	winter
snake	times	wished
snow	tired	woke
soccer	to	wolf
soft	together	woman
someone	too	woods
soon	top	world
stars	toy	would
started	tried	wouldn't
stay	trip	
still	true	year
stop	trunk	yellow
stopped	try	
street	turned	
suddenly		
summer	ugly	
Sunday	under	
supper	until*	
sure	upon*	
	use	
tail		
talk	visit	
team		
teeth	wagged	
television	walked	